THE UNPERFECT MARRIAGE

THE UNPERFECT MARRIAGE

Liberation for couples trapped in the fantasy of perfection

Phillip and Darlena Fields

XULON PRESS

Xulon Press
2301 Lucien Way #415
Maitland, FL 32751
407.339.4217
www.xulonpress.com

The Unperfect Marriage
Liberation for couples trapped in the fantasy of perfection

Printed in the United States of America.

ISBN-13: 978-1-6305-0234-8

TABLE OF CONTENTS

————⋘⟡⋙————

ABOUT THE AUTHORS

Hey! Thanks for taking a peek inside our book. In America, it's typical common courtesy to introduce yourself to a person before you start spilling your guts to them. You know, like you would the hairdresser doing your cut and color, the person seated next to you on a long plane ride, the Uber driver…get the picture?

So, this is, Phillip—a big football player kinda guy with a big heart raised in Chester, VA, as the son of a blue-collar trucker, who leveled-up his life to become a successful marriage & family counselor; sought-after, leadership coach and speaker/teacher. And this is, Darlena—a fiery little gal from the big state of Texas; where she grew up in a trailer on a horse farm, as the daughter of small-town business owners; who has pressed on to create a life she loves as spiritual mentor, life coach…and party planner!

We've been married 27 years and currently live in Senoia, GA. Together we have a non-profit, Get Real Ministries and coaching business, Be Courageous. We consider ourselves to be transformation specialists and live to see lives transformed. But, the joy of our lives is our three stunning, greathearted daughters, Andelyn, Lydia and Darcy; and fun-loving, tenderhearted son, Wilson.

We're about to tell you the messy middle of our lives—how through grit, guts and grace, we went from those lonely, small-town, blue-collar kids to where we are today. But don't worry we're not just going to puke on you emotionally, bolt, then leave you shocked in your airplane seat. We are braving our story with vulnerability, because we've learned that true freedom comes from setting others free. Our hope is that by sharing our UNperfect story you will find the hope and courage to embrace the unperfectness of your own story and hear, "You are not alone."

CULTURE THAT PROPAGATES THE FANTASY OF PERFECTION

What do you see when you are standing in the checkout line at the grocery store? You see perfection personified. The appeal to be perfect glares at you through (slightly altered) pictures on the front of magazines as you stand there checking out. What are these pictures saying to you? If you could have the perfect body, perfect garden, perfect vacation home, perfect sex life, or the perfect children then you could feel good about yourself. You would be an American idol if you were perfect.

The promise of perfection is not attainable and marketing executives know it. They aren't selling perfection. They are selling the fantasy of perfection. The lure is the feel-good promise that when you take the bait and buy into the lie, then you will feel so much better about yourself. The problem is that chasing the fantasy of perfection leads to a very distorted understanding of reality. We get hooked believing that without obtaining the fantasy, we are never good enough. Our inadequacy drives us to chase for something to hide behind or to prop us up so that we don't feel wimpy and meaningless.

Our culture judges our struggles. Christian culture is no different and, in some ways, worse. We hammer people with criticism for their struggles. In some ways, we foster hiding and performing for acceptance in the church.

Together, we have spent our entire lives, since we were first saved in our teens, trying to be perfect enough for our families, for the church, for our peers, for each other, and for God. We've swung between the extremes of being too much to not enough all our adult life as we tried to make it on staff at churches and fit into the stereotypical Christian culture—to belong. For one church, we were too radical and the next church not biblical enough. Another church, we were too charismatic and the next we were not happy enough. After years of pleasing, perfecting, performing, and many times, hustling to get it right, we've come to the conclusion that we are enough.

We are enough to Jesus and we are enough to each other.

We belong to Him and to each other and that is enough. Anyone or any place that's looking at performance from us anymore is going to find themselves disappointed, staring at their watch, and waiting until the cows come home. We're D-O-N-E, done!

Chapter 1

THE FANTASY BEGINS

Childhood Stories: Phillip's Disney Family Story

"**D**amn it, woman! I told you to get my food on the plate!" Dad's voice echoed through the house like a drill sergeant. "I'm coming," Mom answered, laboring to get his plate fixed.

She hurried to the den where he sat isolated, perched in his over-sized comfy chair, and glued to his old western cowboy show blaring on the TV.

Mom arrived with a hot plate of southern fried crispy chicken legs, fried taters, onions, and a mess of fresh snapped green beans cooked in bacon grease. Dad jerked the hot plate from her hand and slammed it down on the TV tray perched on his lap. Some of the greasy food slid off the plate. He looked up at her as if she were to blame for ruining his meal.

"Now look at what you did, stupid!" he bellowed, always blaming her for everything.

Mom instantly tried to fix it.

"Here let me get it up," she spoke as if she were guilty for making the mess.

She was always pathetically apologetic.

He snapped!

He angrily flipped the plate up and yelled, "Just get the hell out of the way!"

Food hurled through the air. Chicken, taters, and green beans exploded across the room, most of it landing all over mom. She tried not to let him see her tears while she hurried to clean up the food.

My brothers and I sat paralyzed at the kitchen table staring at our food and looking up occasionally. We didn't know what to say. My oldest brother took the protector role. He made sure we were safe. My middle brother was the protestor. He hated injustice like a shot in the arm. No one was going to hurt him or someone he cared about without paying the price. I was the runner. Anytime shizzle hit the fan, I bolted out the door, the room, or the situation as fast as I could. Fear triggered me and my go-to reaction was to escape.

I grew up watching dad dominate mom over and over. She was his servant. He controlled her every move with his anger. He barked orders and she jumped up to please his every command. Mom was petrified that he would escalate into a house destroying rage at any given minute if she didn't do exactly what he demanded. My mother's mission in life was to please my father and make him happy. She was rarely successful.

They grew up in coal mining country right on the border of the Virginia-West Virginia line. Mountain living was cruel for poor people like my parents. Having a job, any job was your only way out. Dad was a high school drop-out who fudged his birth certificate to enlist in the army. The only thing he knew how to do was to work hard. He was more afraid of failing than exhausting himself. Nobody could tell him anything different because he was going to do it his way. Mom was a real coal miner's daughter. Her daddy spent the better part of his life miles underground in mine shafts. Mom was pure and sheltered from the real world.

My parents met at a skating rink where dad started putting on his charm. Shortly after courting my mom, dad stole her away from her family. He wooed her away from her family and real life started. He was a hard-working truck driver and mom was a part-time anything that paid for milk money. Dad was desperate to prove himself by finding a job that took him away from his miserable hard-driving life.

I remember the day that changed my life like it was yesterday. The food went flying and dad was in a rage. He sprang to his feet and grabbed mom by the hair in one motion while roaring at the top of his voice.

"How many times have I told you to get out of way I don't need no woman doing anythang for me-ya dumbass!"

My brothers bound up from the table like they were going to a fire drill. They ran toward the fire and I ran to save myself. The sound of my dad's hard fist smashing against my mother's delicate face was too much for me to bear. I ran with tears streaming down my face and panic racing through my body.

Who can save me from this never-ending nightmare?

My eight-year-old mind carried me to the only place I could think to run. I knew my best friend, Jimmy, could help me. The tar and rock road gashed into my bare feet as I ran as fast as I could. A block felt like ten miles. Sweat poured down my face, the tears were drying up, but I was out of breath.

I thought to myself, "I can't go pounding on the door, they will know something is up." I made a quick assessment of the situation. "If I tell the truth, then his parents could find out and that could lead to a beating for me. So, I will sneak up on them and see if the coast is clear," I reasoned as I edged my way up to the house.

It was a blustery mid-summer Sunday night in central Virginia in the '70s. People were doing family time. Jimmy and his family, which included his dad, mom, and a little sister, were gathered together in their sunken den which was part of the split-level house in our blue-collar neighborhood.

Time froze. I was mesmerized into a hypnotic trance. I stared in the window as nightfall surrounded me. There they were, sitting together around the TV with perfect little TV-trays and properly pro-portioned Swanson TV-dinners with the little chocolate brownies tucked in the right corner of the meal container.

"Oh my gosh," they were watching my favorite Walt Disney classic, *Mary Poppins*, about the super happy and always charming lady who took over the room with her witty sense of humor and her nurturing nature.

"This is what a perfect family looks like," I thought to myself. All of them were bubbly and laughing together in pure harmony. There was no shouting or arguing about anything because everybody acted like best friends. They always had fun together watching their favorite shows and eating their pre-packaged ready-made meals. There was no anger, no crying, and no sadness. Life was bliss for Jimmy's family.

That was my first taste of the fantasy of perfection.

I vowed to myself in that moment, "I'm gonna have myself a perfect family." That thought was tattooed on my soul and the fantasy began. The revelation came to me that if I found the right girl then I could have the perfect family. I needed someone like Mary Poppins to rescue me. I could possess my perfect family someday if I could find my Mary Poppins. That girl would erase all the pain and misery from my childhood, and we could live happily ever after.

However, my model for marriage was broken. Men were beasts whose uncontrollable urges enslaved women. Women were subject to a miserable long life of service because society and religion say they "have to." The real movie that portrayed marriage in my mind was "Beauty and the Beast." Men are in charge and dominate women who must perform for love.

My life's goal was to be a better man. I didn't want to control and manipulate my wife with the threat of physical force or emotional manipulation. I was going to prove myself by being a good husband. I wanted to be a sensitive, caring gentleman that took care of his wife and family. I wasn't going to repeat my father's mistakes.

I remember daydreaming in the back seat of the car of a Baptist deacon who picked me up on Sunday mornings. The neatly dressed man loved on his wife who sat next to him in the front seat of the family size station wagon as he drove to church. I promised myself when I got married someday, I was going to sweet talk my wife like that godly man did to his wife and give her little gentle pats on the shoulder during our conflict-free conversations.

At the time, though, I didn't realize how much pain I was carrying. I was deeply wounded and desperate to be loved. I would do anything to please others hoping my perfect behavior would turn into emotional strokes. The nice little boy who would do extra chores for neighbors and spoke with polite manners was me.

I would never be guilty of abusing my fantasy wife like dad treated mom. I was a man with a plan. My charisma would woo her and my hard work would win her respect. She would make her life about pleasing me because I was such a great leader devoted to God. No, my demands wouldn't be enforced with the threat of abuse. I was much more Christian than that. True love would be our reason for serving one another.

Daydreaming of the perfect wife and the perfect marriage would lead to the perfect family. Freedom from the shame of my childhood was my obsession. I hated the way I felt as a young boy. I hated the way my dad treated my mom.

**Deep desperation painted the image
of my make-believe marriage in my head.**

As a result, I set the bar for expectations so high, a woman couldn't jump over it if she was part kangaroo. If we were going to church, then she needed to be super-spiritual. If we were making love, then she needed to be hot and sexy. If she was cleaning the house, then it needed to be spotless. If she was taking care of the kids, then she needed to be supermom. The endless check-list fabricated my fantasy.

The perception I conjured up for my future wife was based on a big fat lie. It was the wife's job to make the man feel important and honored. Her willingness to fulfill every detailed expectation on my checklist would be a sign that she loved and respected me. It was her fault if I felt unimportant.

There was something wrong with this picture. The marriage was doomed before we got started. The problem wasn't with the bride and her inability to fulfill my need to become a man. My fantasy was the problem. The fantasy was, if my wife performed her wifely duties with perfection, then I could feel like a man. If I couldn't manipulate her to make me feel like a man, then I don't have what it takes to be a man. It's no wonder I was extremely disappointed that my marriage didn't turn out the way I planned for it to be.

Childhood Stories: Darlena's Country Club Story

I was taught how to hide behind perfection real good growing up in a small town in Texas. My family owned the largest manufacturing jewelry business in the Northeast part of the state. Everyone for miles around knew who we were because of our large retail storefront and the business advertisement that previewed every movie at the local theater. By day, we were a well-to-do family with expensive clothes, cars, a lake house, boats, a horse farm, and racehorses. But by night, it was hell-behind-closed-doors with drunken brawls, screaming and yelling, gun threats, and many times running for your life. This craziness didn't just involve my family, but included my grandfather (Papaw), my step-grandmother (Ninnie), along with my aunt, uncle, and cousin who lived on a shared property in top-of-the-line, bricked-in, mobile homes within spittin' distance of each other. We owned the local trailer park, too. Yeah, we lived high-on-the-hog.

My Papaw, my paternal grandfather, was in charge of our redneck dynasty, calling all the shots. In other words, he hollered, "Jump!" and we asked, "How high?" He insisted on the whole family, all nine of us, cramming around a table for six, in his tiny, trailer house kitchen, most every night for dinner. That was where the ruckus typically got started after Papaw was "three sheets in the wind." He inevitably would start something with my momma, whom he loved to hate. He hated her, because he couldn't break her and felt intimidated by her, yet he loved her because she made him look good.

Papaw, who to this day is one the most artistically ingenious people I've ever met, could make something out of nothing like nobody I've ever seen. He proudly began the family business all by himself with only a sixth-grade education. He was forced to drop out of school during The Great Depression to go to work and help support his family, which his drunk of a father had left to starve.

On the other hand, Momma was intelligent, dignified, spoke well, and had business savvy. In fact, she would've won valedictorian of her senior class if they'd given those kinds of awards to girls who were married at sixteen. Yep, my momma ran away from home in the middle of the night, after her step-dad beat her with his belt buckle and broke her ribs. She eloped to Oklahoma to marry my eighteen-year-old daddy, but that's a side-story for another day. Back to Papaw picking fights with my mom.

Without fail, when Papaw was done with dinner, he'd push away from the table, undo his pants with his big gut hanging out and start joking with people. The jokes would soon turn into jabs. Then, like clockwork, it was fightin' time. Everyone would square off and take their places, like they were their assigned roles in a soap opera. Momma would stand up to Papaw. He would threaten to hurt her or worse. Daddy and Ninnie would start their peace-making attempts, which sounded more like ass-kissing. My aunt and uncle would slip out the back door, incognito, once the threatening commenced. I would get my little brother and sister, walk them home (just across the yard), where I could keep them quiet and protect them from being harmed.

On occasions when things were really rough, I'd tuck my siblings safely away and jump right in the big middle of the brawl in an attempt to protect Momma from the blows. I was my Papaw's little princess, so he wouldn't dare hurt me and I trusted in that. He paraded me everywhere, spoiled me by buying me everything, and treated me as if his joy hung on my little finger. I adored him because he treated me like a princess, yet at the same time feared him because he threatened my momma's life. I wanted to be with him all the time, while keeping a knife between my mattresses to kill him if he hurt her. Ours was a classic grandpa-who-thought-his-granddaughter-hung-the-moon-but-abused-her-mother-relationship. It was very twisted.

My poor dad was a small man who had a childhood like the Johnny Cash song, *A Boy Named Sue*. He grew up fighting to defend himself. Because my Papaw was at the top of the food chain in our family, calling all the shots and keeping everyone under his thumb with his dominion, Daddy was a "man" at home. He lived shut-down until he walked in the door of our house. My experience with him was like this until my late teens, with memory clips of him being very comical and silly on occasion. He was what you'd call a rage-a-holic, but what endeared me to him in spite of his rage, what his humble apologies. I knew somehow without him ever saying it that there was repressed rage inside of him every waking moment. He was constantly fighting the monster that he hated. I would come to understand my daddy in a very deep way with age.

We lived on the edge of town with our fancy mobile home estate on one end of the property, the horse farm at the other end, and the trailer park in between. Sometimes, we'd have to escape out the back door of our trailer and run straight through that trailer park to the barn. We'd hide there until all the slamming, banging, and yelling quieted, and the gunfire ceased. That was our way of knowing Papaw had passed out.

However, not one time did anyone ever stick their head out of their trailer house to ask if we were okay or call the police as we tip-toe-ran by their homes. I know they had to have heard all the carrying on and gunfire. I guess they were hiding out, too, scared for their lives. Not only were we taught to hide our crazy family dysfunction back in the day, but we were also taught to mind your own business no matter how bad it got.

Momma, bless her heart, hustled to keep us dressed in the best, drive the best, and be the best at everything in an effort to help us feel normal. However, at the end of the day, she really pushed for all that perfection in an effort to hide our private hell and keep the family looking good to the public eye. So, you could say I grew up feeling like trailer trash with a bow on it.

Here's the real kicker, though. Everyone in my family lived in fear that someone would get hurt or maybe even killed during those nightly battles. You want to know what was even more terrifying to my family? What we were all truly haunted with was not the fear of losing our life, but the sheer terror of losing our reputation. The fear of other people finding out who we really were, in other words, our cover being blown. It was unthinkable that our family might be pub-licly exposed and our small empire come tumbling down.

For us Drake's, it would have been more honorable to die than to be found out.

Because my home life was so volatile, I had a very intense fantasy life to help cope. It helped keep me from going bonkers in the controlled chaos I lived in. I spent hours fantasizing about the lives of the popular kids, their ski vacations in Colorado over Christmas break, beach vacations in Florida during spring break, their lake houses where they spent every weekend waterskiing during summer break, and about how much fun it must have been to go to summer camp without their parents. I was certain their lives were just like I saw on my T.V. shows, *Leave it to Beaver, The Brady Bunch,* or *Eight is Enough.* I rarely got to go to friends' homes because my daddy didn't trust anyone not to kidnap me and hold me for ransom. It baffled me what he thought I could possibly be exposed to considering all I witnessed at home, along with his fetish for the horror movies he let us watch with him. However, if my friends' parents passed a criminal background check, Daddy then interviewed their pastor, and I was allowed a rare visit to a friend's home. When this happened, I was enthralled with how happy and peaceful they seemed. Their homes were picture-perfect!

The memory that's seared in my brain and sparked within me an intense longing for a different life, happened when I was in middle school. An incident took place on a Saturday afternoon, during summer break. A friend called to invite me to go swimming with her at the local country club where everybody who was anybody was a member, except my family, of course! We were just redneck wealthy, not the country club kind, even though my family did put their money in a bank and not stashed inside a coffee can buried in a hole dug in the backyard.

The phone my friend was calling from must have been near the pool because I could clearly hear laughter and water splashing in the background. With a sorrowful heart, I had to tell her I couldn't come. I was ashamed that I was stuck at home babysitting my brother and sister, like I did most every Saturday.

She pleaded, "Awe come on, *eeeeeveryone* is here."

I never got to go. Not even once. My parents' business was open on Saturdays and I was expected to pull my weight. After I hung the phone up that day, a deep resentment oozed into my heart against my highly controlled life. I vowed right then and there, that I'd have the perfect country club life someday. No one would ever control me! When I got old enough to have a choice, they certainly would never keep me from missing out on anything ever again. Along with the resentment and the vow, a tormenting fear of missing out on whatever everybody who was anybody was doing took up residence in my soul.

Fear of missing out is actually a legit thing that many people struggle with, I've discovered, with my teenagers' help. It's so much a thing, that it has its own acronym—FOMO. It's a thing so intense, I still battle with it today on big partying holidays or special occasions, like New Year's Eve, the 4th of July, or Super Bowl.

It was this moment that set in motion my search for the perfect guy to help make my Country Club dreams come true.

He would be rich and gorgeous with a nice butt, wear Wranglers and boots, drive a jacked-up truck and have a souped-up muscle car for cruising the strip. H would be from a country club family that owned a lake house and ski boat, and lastly, be a member of the Baptist Church where all good folks went on Sunday mornings in their dress-up clothes. I wasn't raised in church, so I thought that's what church people did.

Do you remember how I said my family had a lake house? Well, I have to confess, it was a dang trailer, too. That was surely not my fantasy, by any stretch of the imagination. In fact, while we're on the subject, I want to let you in on another, not quite as significant vow that I made to myself. I promised myself, that if I ever got to leave that cracker box on wheels that I grew up in, I would NEVER, EVER live in a trailer house again. File that away for later.

Summary

We both started building fantasies in our minds of what happy and loved looked like from an early age. The fantasies were created to take us away from the misery we felt as kids. Both of us were abusively controlled as children. The early years set in motion desperation to find love and belonging. Neither of us realized how much the pains of childhood dominated our perception. We thought the fantasies were normal desires. Fantasies were created because our normal was crazy, but we didn't realize that was unhealthy.

What were your childhood fantasies built around?

How did these fantasies affect your relationship expectations as you moved into your teenage and young adult years?

Did you set the bar for expectations so high no one could fulfill them?

Did you develop a fear of missing out—FOMO—on whatever everybody who was anybody was doing?

How did this fear affect your relationships before marriage?

Chapter 2

MEET MRS. RIGHT AND MR. PERFECT

Darlena: Love at First Sight Story

B efore I can explain how Phillip and I met and fell in love, which is a story I love to tell, I first have to share how a little Texas chick and a big Virginia guy wound up in the same place to even be able to meet. So, I will begin by reminding you of how I spent hours upon hours daydreaming and fantasying about a perfect life as a little girl to cope with my environment—a life so much bigger, vibrant, and far removed from my small, oppressed one that I knew.

One of those dreams was how my personal, handsome prince would gallantly ride into town on a white horse, in his wranglers and boots to rescue me. Once he did, we would ride off into the sunset and live in the proverbial happily-ever-after bliss that most little girls dream of, just like in the Disney movies. Except, I really did need a rescuer to come for me or at least a little help from someone with a great escape plan. Even just a white horse to carry me away into the sunset to Dreamland would do.

As time inched closer to my senior year of high school, I grew more and more hopeless of ever leaving that small town or my trapped life, much less find my handsome prince. As far as I could surmise from what my daddy was letting on, I was going to live at home after graduation, commute to the nearby junior college, study business, marry my drug-head boyfriend he had trained to be a jeweler, get our own fancy, bricked-in trailer within spittin' distance of my parents, and run the family jewelry business. This plan did not have happily ever after written anywhere in the fine print. Even though wild horses couldn't drag me away from my high school sweetheart, he was not my dream. That plan my daddy had devised was not what I had fantasized. It was not even close. Even so, I believed that the plan was as good as it would get for me and all that I deserved.

**Just when I thought all my dreams were lost
in the smallness of that despairing plan,
Jesus came and rocked my world!**

You see, Momma got radically saved. I mean radical, like prayer-walking around drug houses, leading hookers to Jesus, throwing away all my "worldly" cassette tapes, and handing me Petra and Resurrection Band in their place. No matter how hard I tried, I just could never get into Christian rock bands. Anyway, my mom started dragging me to church with her in spite of my obvious hangovers. If that wasn't bad enough, she made me leave my drug-head boyfriend for an entire week to go to church camp!

I might have daydreamed about what it would be like to get to go to summer camp when I was little, but not when I was a too-cool-for-school, almost senior. Not only had I gotten too cool, but I had serious things going on that I couldn't leave, like cruising main street twenty times a night, smoking pot in the hang-out parking lot, and fooling around in the backseat of my boyfriend's '80s Trans Am.

**My mother didn't care a bit about my protests.
She was on a mission from God.**

She packed my bags, shoved me in her Lincoln Continental Mark V, slammed the door shut, spun off, with gravel slinging and dust flying everywhere, while my mouth was hanging open in minor shock. It was quite the move, kind of like a get-away scene out of a movie! I was actually quite impressed, yet super pissed about my predicament. Turns out, my mom knew what she was doing by forcing me to go to that summer church camp, because it was as that very camp where I too got radically saved.

I held off until the very last night of camp—the final hour. I stayed pissed about being there pretty much the whole week and was spewing my rebellion all over everyone that came near me. I'll confess that it was dang hard to keep my insulation up. The night services were pure torture. That preacher was singing my song and tugging at my heart like I had never experienced before. I will never forget him. His name was Louis Torres, a former member of a gang in New York that the book, *The Cross and The Switchblade*, was written about.

Come Friday night service, he was pouring it on thick and his story was ripping my heart out. I couldn't take it anymore. I felt like if he didn't hurry up and give that altar call, I was going to catapult straight out of my chair, bypass the aisle, and land face first on the makeshift altar! Finally! He gave the appeal. I don't even remember how I got there, but I a face-planted on that stage, hair all over, tears squirting uncontrollably, snot pouring, body convulsing, and gave my whole heart and soul, plus all my dreams, to Jesus.

You could say that it was a full-body conversion.

Once I got all my confessions and dreams out, a joy like I had never known hit me like a lightning bolt, and I burst into full-blown, belly laughing for no apparent reason, other than a Jesus Himself rushed into my soul and obliterated all the darkness with His marvelous light. I literally laughed for hours and woke up with my stomach muscles sore and my eyes puffed shut. I had never felt such a state of peace when I opened my eyes the next morning. The dawn of new hope rose over my pitiful little life. I had an inkling that something good was going to happen to me, just like jolly Mr. Roberts always said on that T.V. show of his, which played in my house every Sunday morning, though nobody watched. I got to unload my heart and soul on that make-shift altar and the God of the universe heard me and saw me.

I began making some drastic life changes when I got home. I got back to being the straight-A, perfect-conduct girl that I had always been before I became a hellion at sixteen. I changed my look and my friend group, started doing my homework again, stopped hating my life, started willingly going to church with my mom, and took up a new hobby of praying for my family. Oh, yes, I dumped my drug-head boyfriend and sought out some decent Christian music, as well. Hello, Amy Grant!

Then, something wildly wonderful happened. My daddy started going to church! Then, Ninnie started joining us, too. Finally, Papa, the patriarch, the hell-starter of our family, began attending, as well. My parents and grandparents either accepted Christ for the first time or dedicated their lives to Christ at a small church that they had passed on their way to our jewelry store for Lord knows how many times.

One day, my momma felt compelled to go inside that little church and her decision changed the whole dynamic of our family and home-life. I'm sure you can understand how this was quite the dream come true for me. Praying became my new, secret super-power. It's like I couldn't get enough of it once I started seeing the results.

Then a miracle happened. I had made one friend at church camp that summer, the one and only girl who was able to reach passed my attitude and touch my heart. Well, she called in the fall, which was my senior year to invite me to an Oral Roberts University college weekend in Tulsa, Oklahoma. Shocker of all shockers, my beyond-strict daddy actually let me go! I was beside myself with excitement at the thought of such a monumental event about to take place in my life! Daddy didn't even run a criminal background check on her or her family. My friend and I, all by ourselves, without parents, drove four hours away from home to ORU. We got to stay in a dorm on campus for two days and two nights, attending workshops, meetings, social events, and chapel services. Every second of the visit was exhilarating. I literally had the time of my life, all seventeen years of it!

When I got back home, my daddy, who rarely ever made conversation with me, asked how I liked ORU. While trying to temper my excitement as I shared how much I loved it, not just liked it, and explained how it would be heavenly to go to school there, he began to cry. My compassionately inquisitive look made way for him to share a story with me that I'd never heard of how he once had a dream of attending school at ORU. Because that dream did not become a reality for him, he prayed that one of his children would get to go to school there. Turns out, it was me! I'd never seen Daddy cry like that, nor had I ever had a conversation like that with him or since then. It was a serendipitous moment that created an endearment between my daddy and me that I still feel to this day, even though he is in a nursing home with Alzheimer's.

That moment of impact also gave an explanation for why, even though we did not go to church or anything else Christian, that Oral Roberts Sunday morning Christian TV program, *Expect A Miracle,* roared loudly every weekend in our tiny bricked-in mobile home. Looking back now, I see how that show playing brought a sense of peace in our home that seemed foreign back then. Which is most likely why it lured me into it when I tried to walk past the T.V.

At the end of every show, Oral would point his giant finger right in the camera and say, "Something good is going to happen to you today!"

I recall standing in my little flowy, white nightgown, right in front of the big, television set, which stood as tall as me on Momma's coveted red shag carpet. I'd get so close that the tip of my itty-bitty nose would touch the screen and I could feel the tingle from it all over my face. I'd wonder if Mr. Roberts with the big finger was talking to me and if anything good would happen for me someday.

**As it turned out,
Jesus ended up being my knight in shining armor.
He rescued me from the life I'd dreamed of escaping
for as long as I could remember.**

Getting plucked out of that little, going-nowhere town and out of my crazy family system, drastically changed the trajectory of my life. If momma hadn't gotten saved, if she hadn't forced me to church camp, I would have never gone to ORU where I first learned of Phillip. I certainly would have never gone to Regent where I made sure we met. I just love how God divinely tweaks, scoots, moves, and sometimes even heave-ho's things around—orchestrating our lives in such a masterfully divine and profound way, causing moments to align providentially! He's so great like that!

Even though Phillip and I both went to college at ORU, we did not meet until we were both at Regent University, where we attended graduate school in Virginia Beach, Virginia. I knew who he was at ORU, but he did not know me. He was the youth pastor at the mega-church my girlfriends and I attended. My roommate had a big crush on him and she would go goo-goo anytime she spotted him. He had a white suit he often wore for Sunday morning service and she would almost pass out when she saw him in that. They actually ended up dating for a little while.

So, when I recognized him on the front steps of Regent University during the first week of school, I thought to myself, "Oh, I know him. He's Pastor Phil. I remember his send-off service to come to school here. I'll have to make sure I get a chance to meet him. We will have so much in common."

I finally accomplished it before the fall semester was over. I arranged for him to pick up something from the student services office on campus (one of my three jobs) the Monday after Thanksgiving Break 1991. He arrived just 5 minutes before my shift ended. I had just stood up from my desk to close up shop when he walked through the double-doored entrance. I locked eyes with his, my mouth fell open, my legs went noodle-y, I got butterflies in my stomach, and it was like everything went slo-mo while "Love is a Many-Splendored Thing" started playing in the background. I suddenly went speech-less. I did not believe in "Love-at-First-Sight" up until this moment of impact, but quickly converted to a firm believer.

To make our meeting event more impactful, I had been dumped by a fiancé a year prior. I was so devastated that I gave a year of my life to the Lord to heal, find myself, and not date. Well, that just happened to be my lucky day—the day my year was up. How crazy, right? Crazy good!

We had our first date a week later. He showed up wearing Wranglers and boots! Now, I have to admit that I had high hopes of being hoisted up into his jacked-up pick-up truck next. However, he walked me out to the parking lot and helped lower me into his little Honda Civic, instead. My disappointment over the car soon melted away by the events that took place next. He had made reservations at a nice restaurant in Williamsburg, Virginia, which was a 45-minute drive. He had plans for us to play a get-to-know-you game. He said we could ask each other any question we wanted, just not the same one.

He went first, asking me about my family. Since I had just had my heart broken into pieces a year prior, I decided to tell him all the dirt on me and my family. That way if he was going to dump me, we could get it over with quickly and painlessly. The guy seriously didn't even flinch at hearing every gritty, grimy thing I could think to say. It made me a little uneasy, honestly. So, I plotted my next chess move. I would ask him to tell me about his purpose and the calling of God on his life. If he couldn't answer flawlessly, that would be reason enough for me to end this thing fast, before it could get started.

Surprisingly, he called my bluff and articulated his calling and purpose without so much as a pause to take a breath. While listening, another moment of impact took place, the God of the universe that listened to me pour out my hopes and dreams at summer camp sprawled out on that stage, decided He had something important enough to say audibly, in my head that is. I guess He did it to make sure I could never question the validity of what He had to say.

**Loud and clear, I heard,
"This is your soul mate, whom I have chosen for you."**

I was completely stunned, to say the least yet trying to show zero emotion. I mean how insane would that have been to gently interrupt and say, "Excuse me, but God just told me you're supposed to be my husband. Got any thoughts about that?" My mind quickly rushed back to my ORU days. I was proposed to about five times by these precious little guys that I would have never even given the time of day, who told me God told them I was the one while I was serving myself tapioca pudding. I wasn't about to repeat the tapioca incident! The rest of the night was just a whirl of emotions that I had to contain.

**The voices of college chaplains ran through my head,
"When you meet the man you're supposed to marry,
you'll just know, that you know, that you know."**

Now, I finally understood what they meant! I'd found the man God had for me, the one whom my soul had been longing for, my handsome prince. I believe the Lord knew I needed to directly hear His voice that night telling me that Phillip was the man He'd chosen for me to marry. So, in the future, when hurricanes hit our marriage and I was tempted to run, I would not be able to deny the certainty of our marriage being meant to be.

Our first date was right before the holidays, so I left to drive home shortly after our date. Well, Phillip must have heard the Lord tell him the same thing, because he took a Greyhound bus all the way to Texas to meet my family. At some point during his visit, when I wasn't around, He asked my parents if he could marry me. Then we drove or more accurately, we floated back to Virginia Beach on cloud nine, completely enamored with each other. Though I never told him my crazy story of God telling me he was supposed to be my husband, we did talk about how we were pretty sure this was it. So, Phillip arranged for us to have pre-engagement counseling soon after returning to school. Did I mention we were both getting our Master's in counseling? Yeah, that explains the unusual emphasis on counseling.

Even though I knew we wanted to marry one another, I did not have a clue that Phillip was scheming behind-the-scenes with my daddy about proposing to me in March. Daddy actually made my ring, making it very special even to this day, and FedExed it to Phillip. He chose a day that we had a four-hour lecture together to do the big deed. However, this day he did not show up, which was very out of character for Phillip. He planted one of his friends in the seat right behind me, to razz me every few minutes and get me worried about where he could be or what could have happened to him. I was a nervous wreck.

During break, this same friend hands me a card in Phillip's handwriting which said, "Go to the front of the building immediately. Your chariot awaits you." I jumped up out of my chair just as the professor dismissed for break, screamed unwittingly loud, "He's going to propose!" Then I took off out of the lecture hall, down the stairs, and out in front of the building with the entire class trailing behind me, where I saw no chariot.

I'm looking side-to-side, beside myself with excitement, when one of my classmates yelled, "The parking lot, idiot!"

So, I ran down the sidewalk and into the parking lot, where a chariot would obviously be able to park, and there sat a white-stretch limo with a chauffeur in a black tux, leaning against it. I walked methodically to the car, as if I'd just learned to use my legs, heart beating out of my chest and eyes wide.

The chauffeur asked, "Do you happen to be Darlena Drake?"

As I slowly nodded, the chauffeur opened the farthest of far back doors and inside sat Phillip, dressed in a black suit. I thought I'd just died and gone to heaven. There was a dozen red roses, a bottle of champagne on ice, and a black dress laying across the seat. Good thing, he had plans to drive me home and change, because I had been awake for about 48 hours working on a term paper. I had on a t-shirt, jeans, tennis shoes with my hair in a ponytail and no make-up. I'm sure I didn't smell all that lovely, either.

He explained on the short ride to my apartment that I had approximately 20 minutes to get ready. I've never before or since gotten ready so fast in all my born days! I showered, shaved, washed, dried and rolled my hair, painted my nails and toes, wiggled myself into that dress, yanked up some black hose, and slipped on my black pumps with seconds to spare.

The chauffeur drove us to a quaint French bistro near the beach. We had a four-course meal in a tiny, private room with a fireplace. I had lobster bisque for the first time in my life, which was heavenly. I love it to this day because it reminds me of that dreamy experience. The waiter was apparently in cahoots with Phillip, because when he leaned down to serve us our dessert, the ring box was sitting on the tray. Phillip grabbed the ring, got down on one knee, and proposed to me right then and there. One of the most thrilling moments of my life.

Then, the chauffeur took us for a drive and allowed me to hang out of the sunroof like Julia Roberts on *Pretty Woman* and yell, "I'm getting married!" as we cruised along the coastline. Every second of the night was perfect and remains etched in my mind! The story of our over-the-top, romantic engagement spread throughout the school and left a legacy for other poor, lovestruck fellows to follow at Regent University for years to come. Directly after our perfect engagement, we began our pre-marital counseling, so we'd be perfectly prepared for our marriage like good little counseling students.

We were doing everything right to prepare for the perfect marriage!

Even having to spend the summer apart was perfect for us getting to know each other more intimately, since we'd only have the phone to keep us connected. He moved to Chicago to begin his new job. I went home to live with my parents in Texas to plan our perfect, fairy-tale wedding. It was all-white, outdoors, on the shore of a lake, with Beauty and the Beast as our theme. I had sixteen girls in my bridal party—eight bridesmaids and eight honorary bridesmaids. I know, right? How ridiculous! He struggled to even find enough guys to be his groomsman, but he had Mr. Wilson for his Best Man, which was the most important thing.

We forgot to plan for the sun going down early when we scheduled the time for our wedding, so it got dark before we could say, "I do." Good thing everyone was dressed in white. Looking back now, I wonder if that wasn't a sign of the dark days awaiting us. If that wasn't crazy enough, I ended up slinging my wedding band off my finger as I was directing everyone where to go and what to do, as I was my own wedding coordinator. I know what you're thinking, "I had to make sure everything was perfect." Guilty as charged! By the time we found my ring, we hadn't had a thing to eat and it was time to leave. So, the first place we went as just-marrieds was Taco Bell. How special!

Phillip: Found the Right Girl Story

Getting hitched to the right girl stayed on my mind all the time when I was in high school. I couldn't allow myself to make any big mistakes that would disqualify me. I vowed to myself that I would not have sex before marriage. Sexual sin was a big no, no. The truth was I was petrified of girls. The defense I held for purity could easily be about my devotion to abstinence. However, I wasn't going all the way with girls because I was afraid to even though I was the captain of the football team. My friends unmercifully teased me for not chasing after the women like they did, but I had to remain pure and ready for Mrs. Right.

The deep insecurity I had was rooted in a very traumatic experience from my childhood.

I loved playing outside when I was a kid. Outdoor life was an everyday adventure for me. I built forts, went fishing, rode bikes all over town, and occasionally created mischief like ringing a doorbell and running away before they answered. I stayed outside from dawn until dusk to escape from the fury of my father who seemed to have endless reasons to be mad about nothing.

My curious adventures often landed me in risky places as a young boy. I found myself at a neighbor's house on the other side of town one day. My run-around buddies weren't available, so I decided to do something different. I went to see an older dude who was about the age of my older brother. The guy's house was unfamiliar to me, but he persistently wanted me to come over. He was very sadistic. He liked to hurt animals and talked tough about war, but his weirdness lured me in for some strange reason. I remember he had a sneaky laugh.

He enticed me into his garage where unbeknownst to me, he set up his rendezvous with little kids. I had no idea what was in store for me that day. I was in the wrong place at the wrong time. It was ugly. He coerced me into various sexual activities that no eight-year-old boy should have to perform. My fear meter went on high alert. Alarms sounded off in both ears, "Get out now." The moment he turned his head, I bolted like Speedy Gonzales. I ran out the back of his garage with my pants down around my ankles. Anxiety pulsated through my body.

My heart was racing as excruciating thoughts ripped through my mind, "What just happened? Did I do something wrong? Am I going to get a beating for this? It's all my fault! I'm not telling a soul about this."

That was my introduction to sex. Shame stained my soul.

The horrific trauma was submerged deep into my subconscious as a secret never to be visited especially with my true love. My takeaway was that if having sex with girls was like this gross encounter, then I wanted nothing to do with it.

The family moved from that neighborhood and we landed next door to some good-hearted people. One day, my new friend's mom invited me to church. I had no experience with church. It was as foreign to me as Chinese food. We were southern fried hillbillies from the mountains of West Virginia. The only time people went to the church-house was to get married or buried.

The little white Baptist church in Chester, Virginia was set in a quaint blue-collar suburb thirty minutes south of Richmond. The floor creaked and cracked as you walked into the vestibule. The wooden pews were hard and cold, but there was something stirring in the air. It was unlike anything I had ever experienced in my short twelve-year-old life. It had the sweetest fragrance I ever encountered. The atmosphere was filled with a mysterious but inviting presence. It was like the smell coming from grandma's kitchen. You didn't know what she was making, but you knew it would be good.

This was my first encounter with real love. This was no high-minded theological concept. Something, somebody was touching me deep down in my soul. Oh my, I wanted to stay there forever.

My spiritual journey launched with a real encounter with the love of Christ. I couldn't explain it, but I knew that someone loved me with a close affection that produced a security in my heart. I went from not knowing of God to knowing He was inside me. The simple supernatural transfer started before I could run to the front of the church to pray. Bam! He showed up and I came alive.

I don't care what skeptics say, Jesus changed my life forever as hope invaded my soul that day.

Now I had someone to protect me from my dad the tormentor. Jesus came into my heart and He made Himself very real to me. I couldn't see Him, but I could feel Him. It was like I had a secret source of security living on the inside of me. His presence was with me during the night terrors and He walked with me throughout the day on my adventures.

My teenage years were spent thinking that I was going to be a pro football star. Football was my passion. I dreamed of being drafted by America's team, the Dallas Cowboys. Playing pro football would secure my chances to find my fantasy girl who looked like a Dallas Cowboy cheerleader. Not only did she need to have a Mary Poppins personality, she also needed to be a hot chick. It was a pipe dream, but I thought it could be my only way out. Everything in my early years was geared toward finding a way out.

Life changed the day my football coach and government teacher pulled me out of class. I naturally thought I was in trouble. They explained that they learned about my home life and wanted to help me. A local community patriarch offered me a place to stay. I didn't care if I had to sleep in a barn on a dirt floor, I was ready to get out.

This was the game-changer.
A God-fearing man heard about my situation
and did something about it.

My rescuer was the retired local high school principal who was devoted to helping teenagers up "fools hill." This compassionate fatherly man gave me a place to live, safe from the warzone of my family. Although he never married, he dedicated his life after WWII to creating a family for young boys like me in his home.

I was like a stray dog at first. I wouldn't allow him to get close to me because trusting him terrified me. I will never forget the first time I stepped into the back of that giant southern home. He placed two giant New York strip steaks on the counter and greeted me with a big smile on his face.

"You like steak?" he said, in his eastern shore gruff accent.

I answered softly, looking at the ground, "Yes, sir."

"Good because we are going to have steak, baked potatoes, and salad for supper."

He tried hard to make me feel welcomed, but I thought to myself that sounds good, but what does he want from me? He insisted I call him by his first name, Wilson. The community knew him as Mr. Crump, but I was privileged to call him Wilson. This was a big lesson in intimacy for me. Learning to submit to him and receive his generosity took a long time. Trusting someone wasn't natural for me because of the damage I carried from my dad.

The struggle to trust eventually
would play a big role in my marriage.

Persistence paid off. Wilson's consistent easy-going ways of helping me won my heart. My orphan spirit was slowly transformed. He gave me everything a teenage boy could want including a customized stereo with a turntable that played my albums. He bought a new bedroom set of furniture and gave me a special bedroom in the two-story giant old white house his father built with his own hands. He bought me an old Ford pickup to drive to school.

More than anything,
he reminded me every day that he believed in me.

He told me, "God told me to look after you, Phillip."

That's what he did. I was in heaven. The fantasy of meeting the right girl and creating the perfect family was within reach after being adopted by this generous man. I headed off to college unaware of how much the hidden pain in my heart was distorting my perception of reality. Idealism dominated my picture of the future. I was going to the right school to meet the right girl so that I could go to work as a pastor for the right church. These accomplishments would secure my worthiness to God and for marriage.

Wilson set me up to go to Oral Roberts University. Somehow, he helped me get a bunch of scholarships. I couldn't believe I was leaving little Chester, Virginia, to go and live in Oklahoma. I was the only child on both sides of my family to go to college. I was scared and excited at the same time.

I was like a kid visiting Disney World when I arrived on the college campus in Tulsa. I spent every waking moment exploring, learning, and growing. I didn't make time for social things. Some of my roommates made fun of me for being too serious about God. My young adult years were spent chasing after God not women. The only girlfriend I had at ORU dumped me because I was too crazy about ministry.

My devotion paid off. I was recruited my freshman year to be a youth pastor at an up and coming church. I loved every minute of it. I was so devoted to ministry that my professors had to talk me into staying in school. If I was going to save the world before supper, then I didn't have time to sit through boring lectures about things that happened centuries ago. I wanted to tell the whole world about Jesus, now.

The ORU years flew by faster than the blink of an eye. I was now on staff of a mega-church in the making. Our little storefront mushroomed into a charismatic church on the move. My fantasy job was becoming a reality, but in the back of my head, I knew something wasn't right. The childhood pain was lurking beneath the surface. Emotional pain has a way of surfacing under stress. My hustle for worthiness to be an up and coming world-changer opened the door for others around me to voice a concern about my hard driving nature. Maybe, being the next Billy Graham wasn't God's plan.

One day, in the middle of a staff meeting, I found myself resigning to return to Virginia to try to heal my aching heart. I was commissioned with my pastor's blessing to return to my family. I was hoping that everyone in my family would be excited to work through the pain we experienced during the ugly years. However, after one meeting with a counselor, the healing process came to a screeching halt for my family. I was not going to stop.

This was an odd season because I wasn't working in the ministry. I felt like a fish out of water. However, I knew that I could not return to ministry until I overcame the torment I felt inside. There was a war going on inside of me. Jesus' love was real, but I couldn't shake this deep sense of inadequacy. The search for answers led me to Regent University. The thinking was I would fix myself while studying about dysfunctional families. Great logic, but reading about myself did not make the pain go away. It stirred it up.

Wilson was a big support during these years, but he didn't know how to coach me through the deeper freedom I desperately needed. One day, I was in a chapel service at Regent and listening to a man tell his story. Clay McLean was a big burly guy with a beard and a deep voice to match. He spoke my language. He played a song called, *All My Wounds Cry Allelujah*. That was the first time I met someone who knew my pain. He wrapped his big arms around me and began to hold me tight. Thus, my healing journey began.

I dated girls on and off at Regent University, but I couldn't find Mrs. Right. Everything changed when I got a phone call from the cutest little Texas gal one day. She was working in student services and said I needed to come to the office to pick up some paperwork. Wow! This little gal was purrrdddy. I was smitten. She was bubbly and super spiritual and drop-dead gorgeous. I wanted to get to know her and that's what I did.

Could this be my little Mary Poppins dressed as a Dallas Cowboy Cheerleader? Weird but that was the magic combination I was searching for. I was in love with her because she made life exciting and revved up my motor. The first time we met, I made her cry. She was working and during the interaction, I nervously blurted out bad news about a mutual friend who was in the hospital. Tears started streaming down her face. She couldn't stop crying because the man was her favorite professor at ORU. I diverted the conversation to something spiritual.

I said, "Hey, let's get together and pray for him."

She calmed down and I landed a date with her without asking her out. Little did she know I didn't have the guts to ask pretty girls to go on a date. She tells it better, but the dating phase was quick and the decision to marry wasn't fast enough for me. A year later, we tied the knot. I knew this was the beginning of my fantasy coming true. She made me feel like a man. I thought I was completely healed and totally prepared to share my life with the girl of my dreams. We stayed at a hotel near the airport to leave for Cancun, Mexico the following morning. We are off to Fantasy Land to begin our perfect marriage.

Summary

Radical conversions altered our destinies. The presence of Jesus gave us a purpose for life. The way the Lord rescued us from our sad starts in life was miraculous. Our lives were deeply impacted by the goodness of God. Mr. Wilson and Darlena's mom made a huge contribution to empower us to launch into early adult life. However, both of us showed up to the dating-marriage phase with high expectations for one another to fulfill our fantasy spouse. Our find-your-mate-checklists were filled in with checkmarks. I was her handsome prince wearing wranglers and sweeping her off her feet. She was my Mary Poppins dressed in a Dallas Cowboy Cheerleader outfit, though she never actually wore that outfit. This was going to be amazing. No one could have convinced us that we were headed for troubled waters. We did everything right to secure a successful life of marital bliss.

Did you have a mental checklist when you were looking for Mrs. Right or Mr. Perfect?

How did your relationship with Jesus affect your perfect spouse checklist?

Trusting someone wasn't natural for Phillip, because of the damage he carried from his dad. The struggle to trust eventually would play a big role in our marriage.

What kind of "baggage" from your past did you bring into your marriage relationship?

In Darlena's family, the love relationships and family roles were twisted. For instance, she took on the role of protecting her mother from her grandfather. Papaw treated her like a princess, but was also the one she had to protect her mom from. This adversely affected her role in the marriage and her expectations of how Phillip should treat her.

How did the roles that you held in your family effect your role in your marriage?

Did you have any past relationships that adversely affected what love looked like for you and your expectations of love?

Chapter 3

PARADISE LOST: WAKING UP IN REALITY

Phillip

We were honeymooning in the tropical paradise of Cancun, Mexico. We had a suite on the top of a luxury hotel furnished with a jacuzzi on the balcony including an elevated terrace overlooking the coral blue ocean. This place was perfect for two newlyweds looking to create a life-long romance.

Darlena

Our first night together was just dreamy. Phillip had put white candles all over the room and romantic music was playing…a night etched in my memory. Everything about our honeymoon was dreamy as well—ten days in Cancun, Mexico, with a balcony that we could pull our bed out on, overlooking the ocean. What a way to begin our perfect life together.

Phillip

Guess what I was thinking about? I had a one-track mind. Sex occupied every square inch of my brain. Food, water, air—nothing else mattered. All I wanted was sex, sex, sex. I was determined to get my prize after waiting twenty-eight years to enjoy sexual intimacy. But there was a fear that taunted me day and night. I was horrified that I did not have what it took to please a woman. I could never muster the confidence to go all the way. No worries, though, it was Darlena's job to pursue me. She was crazy about me.

The big day for the bride is the wedding, but for the groom, he is focused on the honeymoon night. All I could think about was how she was going to pleasure me. All the yucky stuff I carried in my teenage years would be erased in one moment. Now, I would feel like a man. It was her responsibility to validate my manhood by fulfilling my lustful pleasures and that would make me feel like I have what it takes to be a man. I'm not saying this was right, but I am admitting how immature my thinking was.

She was the pursuer and I was the happy recipient. The idea of a woman being hot for a man was painted in my mind from watching movies like "Dirty Dancing" and "Grease." My immature mind was filled with images of women acting hot and heavy for the leading men in these movies. I literally thought this is how my wife would act when we were in the bedroom.

My twenty-eight-year-old mind was stuck in a memory from being forced into sex when I was preyed upon by an older teenager in his garage. The impact of that childhood experience was now manifesting. The shame of the past paralyzed me. I didn't know what to do.

My passivity turned into an expectation for my wife. I was assuming that she knew what to do to make the bad memories go away.

My desperation to feel like a man and to prove my manhood set us up for colossal conflict.

Every move she made was under the microscope. If she didn't come after me like a tigress chasing her prey, then I pouted and acted like a teenage boy who was rejected. The woman of my dreams was reduced to a sex object. I gauged my security on her excitement to be with me.

The big blow-up happened and it sent me into a tailspin. It didn't happen in the bedroom. It was our last day in paradise. The disagreement started in the gift shop of the hotel. Darlena demanded to buy souvenirs for all her relatives in Texas.

It sounded like she was saying, "I'm going to buy gifts for my family whether you like it not."

Did I mention that she was buying **her** side of the family presents with my money without my permission? Not on my watch! I pushed back hard at the absurdity of this issue. It was a waste of hard-earned money to buy cheap gifts that would be stuck on a shelf, I told her. She raised her voice and put me in my place by calling me selfish and stupid. Her argument was giving gifts was her love language. *That's just her getting her way,* I thought to myself. I retreated to my childhood. I walked out of the store in protest. *Maybe if I act hurt and pitiful, I can get my way,* I reasoned. I couldn't believe she disrespected me by raising her voice and disobeying me.

Do you see my problem? It's wasn't about buying or not buying gifts. Gifts are special. Fear manifested in typical reactions for both of us. The issue was that I was trying to control her by walking away and she was trying to control me with an angry aggressive tone. Her angry reaction was part of the problem. But my struggle was a deep-seated belief that the only way I get to feel like a man is for my wife to do everything the way I wanted her to do it.

The ridiculous argument over souvenirs messed with my thinking. I had this belief that perfect couples never argue and agree on everything. Her push back and overreaction was too much for me. The strength to be an assertive secure man was non-existent at that point in my life. But I thought it was my wife's fault because she disrespected me.

Something was wrong in paradise. I allowed the hurt from this to fester. This was the beginning of returning to an old sin pattern in my life. I struggled with acting out sexual desires when I felt deep anxiety. Rather than going to my wife with my sexual urges, I turned inward. I didn't consciously realize it then, but I was shutting down toward her after the first month of marriage.

Darlena

Funny thing is I barely even remember that souvenir shop or the incident that Phillip is referring to. Most likely because I got my way and bought the souvenirs that I wanted. Isn't it intriguing, though, how certain situations may deeply impact your spouse, yet barely phase you?

It's all about the paradigm built in us from our upbringing that determines the lenses we view our spouses through and how we experience our marriage.

I knew the honeymoon phase was over a couple of months into our marriage. Phillip's new job after finishing his Master's was at a mega-church in the suburbs of Chicago. He was hired to serve as youth pastor and launch a counseling program. In theory, everything about living in the big city of Chicago as newlyweds and launching a new program at this big tele-evangelist's church seemed thrilling. Why wouldn't I think that after the pastor of this big church took the entire leadership staff on an all-expenses-paid, one-week vacation to a Disney World and Epcot, putting us up at the Dolphin Hotel the day after we arrived?

However, it didn't take long for the thrill to turn into a chill. All that was cold, harsh, and unfamiliar about living there came creeping in around all me screaming, "You don't belong here!" My heart began to yearn for home and all that was familiar, yet home seemed to be getting blown farther and farther away by the bone-chilling winds of the windy city in the dead of winter.

After the new wore off at church and the staff went back to their "normal" selves, all their warm fuzzies turned into cold shoulders. Their behavior didn't help me feel accepted by the church leadership and I certainly didn't feel like I fit in. Without a doubt, I did not belong in Chicago and it was obvious! In fact, I was shocked that I could still be in the U.S. It felt more like I was in a foreign country because the culture was so drastically different from what I was accustomed to. I got "go-to-hell" looks when I was friendly to strangers, drivers honked at me ferociously, and others just cussed me out or flipped me the bird for simply looking at them. Where I was from, folks only honked as a friendly gesture to say hi (emphasis on the "i" in a typical southern draw). I began to feel darkness start to form a familiar cloud over me from the drastic culture change I was experiencing as a Southern Belle in the cold north.

The wind chill was slowing beginning to creep into our little love nest, as well. One night, Phillip wanted sex and I told him that I didn't feel like it. If I'd only known what consequences would follow from turning him down, I certainly would have sucked it up and faked it! Out of his feelings of rejection and disappointment, he spouted off that I'd deceived him into thinking that I was someone that I wasn't. You see, we fooled around quite a bit while dating, basically doing everything but… I had been sexually active before we married, but Phillip was still a virgin. Frankly, I taunted the heck out of him to fool around with me until he caved. It must have happened enough to give him the idea that I was quite the sex kitten. So, I guess, he fully expected me to turn into a tiger once we were married.

What he didn't know and what I didn't realize at the time, was I'd learned that giving guys what they wanted sexually kept them around. In a sense, you could say that having secured my man with a wedding ring, took all the adrenaline rush out of doing something forbidden without getting caught. So, I admittedly agree now that my desires for sexual activity did change drastically after marriage. I can see how he thought I had "deceived" him. However, in that moment, his words were like a dagger in my heart. Shame washed over me and lies took up residence in my soul: "You are a disappointment, therefore, you are unworthy of love."

I had become a disappointment to my man, the new church, and all of Chicago. Add in the homesickness and depression that came banging on the door of my soul. The sex kitten had gotten lost in the snow of cold Chicago. However, I wasn't going to let depression take me down without a fight. I was determined to find her and bring her back home. So, I layered up thick to protect myself from the sting of the below-zero cold while I searched for her. When I opened the door to set foot outside, the fierce, arctic winds blew me over almost instantly. I crawled back inside in defeat. Full-blown depression barged right in and took over. I tried desperately to hide it from Phillip, my family, and my friends back home. I couldn't let Phillip know that his disappointment had gotten the best of me. I was too ashamed to tell anyone back home that my newly married life in Chicago completely sucked!

I was not working or in school but staying at home by myself for the first time in my life. Phillip and I thought it would be a great idea for me to stay home for my first few months to enjoy being a wife, build our little love nest, and acclimate myself to our new life. It would just be for the fall semester, then I'd start back to school in the spring. However romantic that might have sounded, this is what that grand little plan looked like in real life. I was literally stuck at home with no car, no bank account of my own, no job, and no family or friends in the frozen tundra, with 20-bazillion geese outside our apartment honking relentlessly day and night. I felt like I was in a foreign, frozen hell!

Yet, I desperately pretended to be the blissfully happy, little wifey-poo that Phillip expected me to be. I would get up with him in the morning, make his breakfast, iron his clothes, and help him out the door. Like clockwork, I'd go straight back to bed after I watched his car leave the parking lot from our third-story apartment window. Then, I'd get up at noon, when my glorious soap operas began. *All My Children, One Life to Live,* and *General Hospital* became my reason for living and the center of my joy. Their actors were my friends and family. I'd come alive for three hours of my day watching these soap operas, dreading 3:00 P.M. when they had to go away and leave me alone in Chicago.

I weirdly spent all weekend missing them, wondering what they were doing. I shamefully couldn't wait for Monday noon to come again when I could disappear in Soap Opera Land. Then dread of all dreads, after the last note of the *General Hospital* theme song ended and the clock struck three, I would jump off the couch like a racehorse leaping out of the starting gate, to squeeze an entire day's worth of responsibilities into three hours before Phillip returned home at 6:00 P.M. I'd scurry to unpack some boxes, put more belongings away in drawers, and hang some pictures on the wall. Then, I'd whip up an impressive meal. While it was cooking, I'd get showered and dolled up. During the time it took him to park the car and walk up three flight of stairs, I'd slap dinner on the table and a smile on my face while simultaneously attempting to disguise my being out-of-breath as excitement to see him, and give the appearance that I'd been hard at work all day, nest-building.

To avoid too much intimacy with Phillip, I started diving into boxes at night after dinner and unpacking while he was home. I thought that if I could dodge one-on-one's as much as possible, I could maybe keep him from detecting my depression. I couldn't handle the pain of disappointing him anymore, so I needed to toughen myself back up. If I was going to get through this successfully, I had to pull back into myself and pull out my independent, badass Texas-self, which I had perfected before I met Phillip. I'd just gotten a little rusty from letting myself get all lovestruck and sappy by the handsome prince. I came from a long line of tough cookies from my momma's side of the family, so I had some great teachers who were pros at not needing men.

However, I was just kidding myself if I thought I had Phillip fooled. He was no dummy. I was obviously behaving out-of-character as far as he knew. Things weren't okay with me or with us, but he was too afraid and enmeshed in his own internal mess to do anything about it. However, he did have the courage to ask me what happened to the girl he married. Ugh! Another dagger and more shame to embed the lies in my soul and make me believe I deserved whatever I got.

Rejection, distrust, and shame moved in with us,
disheveling our little love nest, unraveling our trust,
and driving a wedge between us
sending us both into hiding and practicing distance.

Disappointment drained all the romance and excitement out of being newlyweds in Chicago. The cold winds slapping us in the face and stepping in goose poop on our way to the car from our apartment had lost its romantic comedy appeal. "Happy ever after" had faded into fake happiness. I couldn't see the country club through the thick, blizzardly snow.

While the northern cold was seeping into the cracks of our would-be love nest, there was a storm brewing at the church. It started when Phillip was asked to use one of the pastor's three, white sports cars to run an errand. He got pulled over while he was out. While shuffling through car papers in the glove box to find the auto insurance for the officer, he noticed that the car was owned by the church. He decided to share his story in the next staff meeting, then proceeded to ask about the cars being in the church's name. Need I say more?

To make matters worse, Phillip was beginning to attract adults from "Big Church" into the youth meeting to hear him teach. As you can probably guess, this wasn't going over too well. We didn't know what to do. Telling the adults to get back into Big Church where they belonged just didn't seem the right way to handle it. So, we just waited it out. This all took place between Thanksgiving and Christmas.

We were required to spend Christmas Eve, Christmas Day, and New Year's Eve at the pastor's house and everything seemed great. It wasn't so great for making memories of our first Christmas season together. I only remember feeling like I was in a Christian adaptation of *The Godfather,* sitting at a ridiculously long table full of Italian people, celebrating the birth of Christ while eating ratatouille, with the pastor seated at the head of the table slinging a glass wine around to toast every few minutes. Everyone would stop to clap and Amen him each time, while waiters swarmed the table with refills. The pastor and staff were all being friendly to us, so we thought maybe they'd decided to discharge the car-questioning incident and forgive Phillip for stealing the congregants from Big Church.

However, the first day back in the office after the holidays, Phillip found an official-looking letter in his staff mail slot from the Church Board explaining a list of stipulations for Phillip to follow in order to remain on the church staff. Number 15 on the list confirmed my gut feelings regarding what the staff thought about me. It read, "Your wife must come out of the youth meetings to attend big church where she will sit on the front row with her Bible, notebook, and pen, and take notes from Pastor R. in order to work out her rebellion." How about that?

On the advice of the Tulsa church pastor, Phillip chose to resign from the Chicago church. Of course, that broke my little heart. **Not!**

This meant we were headed back down south, where I fit like a glove! With the help of my mom, who boarded a plane and flew for the first time in her whole life, God love her, and our youth volunteers, we had a U-Haul rented, packed, and ready to roll by the following weekend. Hallelujah! Thank the Lord! Chicken fried everything, here we come!

It was unfortunate that we had to leave that church the way we did, but I could not have been happier about leaving cold Chicago. I was grateful to be from the south after spending a winter there and happy to say, "Chicago is a nice play to visit, but you wouldn't want to live there." As we drove across the Illinois state line, I prayed that just as we were leaving behind the frigid weather, that we would also leave behind the frigidness that had crept into our marriage. Maybe we could have a sort of do-over once we had a new place to make a fresh start and get back to being the perfect little couple. I also forgave the church for rejecting us because we were not perfect enough for them. I also had to forgive all the people that cussed me, flipped me off or honked at me, which of course lead to me praying that I would never, ever have to hear honking people or honking geese. If I never heard another goose or stepped in goose poop again in my life, it would be too soon!

Summary

A gorgeous tropical honeymoon doesn't guarantee a tight marital bond. Disappointment quickly set in when we didn't live up to one another's fantasies. We went from the bliss of paradise to living disenchanted life in a matter of a few months. When we didn't experience the fulfillment of our fantasies, we turned away from one another and returned to familiar patterns. We weren't getting what we wanted. I wanted her to make me feel like a man and she wanted me to make her feel like a princess. I wanted her to be a sex-kitten, who revved up my motor every night and she wanted me to be a good ole, rich southern boy with a country club membership. We projected our disappointments at one another which started to create distance and disconnection in our marriage.

Did you experience disappointments and unmet expectations once the honeymoon was over?

Did those disappointments begin to create distance and disconnection in your marital relationship?

How did your perception of your spouse change after the early disappoints happened?

Chapter 4

G-RATED DISNEY CLASSIC TO AN R-RATED HORROR SHOW

Darlena

Heading back down south meant beloved Tulsa, Oklahoma, for us. Hallelujah! We were back in the friendly south, where folks are as sweet as the tea, everyone smiles at you, waitresses call you sweetie-pie, and it's not weird to hug or shoot the breeze with strangers. I was back where I felt at home. I was also back in driving distance to my family in Texas, with friends just down the road, and my favorite places to eat and shop just around the corner.

You see, Tulsa was our old college town, where I spent a fun-filled five years at Oral Roberts University. Tulsa and ORU were very special to me for a couple of reasons. First and foremost, ORU was the university that God miraculously opened the door for me to attend. Remember my childhood story and how strict my dad was? Well, he actually let me go to school there, even though it was a whole four-hour drive from home. It's a great little story that's worth telling, but we'll save it for another time.

For me, coming back to Tulsa was like swallowing one big anti-depressant! It helped me find myself again. Maybe that part of me that got frozen in cold Chicago was able to thaw out back in the warm south. Both of us were in hog heaven to be back where everything was familiar. It was full of good memories, close, family friends, and where you could get BBQ anytime you wanted! In fact, we lived with those close friends for our first three months back. Things were great between Phillip and me while living with them. Those were peaceful, fun times, full of moments to reminisce with these dear friends. But then we moved into our own apartment. That began the slow fade.

The lead pastor of the mega-church in Tulsa, OK, where Phillip had youth pastored during his years at ORU, advised us to leave Chicago and move back to work for him again. However, here was no job opening for Phillip in Tulsa, as promised. Thankfully, there was a job opening for me, and not just any ordinary job. It seemed like the perfect job for me and I was super excited that I would actually get to use my degree! However, I felt I had to hide my excitement because Phillip was so downtrodden over the disappointing news of no job.

So, our roles kind of flipped, you could say. I went to work while he stayed home. He spiraled into a funk, while I was soaring with value and significance from my newfound career as a Birthmother Counselor with the church Adoption Agency. I was dressing up for work every day, carrying a pager 24/7, bringing home the bacon, frying it up in a pan like an "Enjoli woman," and probably flaunting it way too much. Phillip was not feeling like much of a man as a stay-at-home-husband. He was looking slouchy, too, and I, of course, let him know with condescending and snarky little remarks. Consequently, the tension in our tiny, one-bedroom apartment was beginning to swell.

He was behaving like a lost puppy, disoriented by the church not hiring him back as he'd expected. He had no Plan B to fall back on, so he was just puttering around trying to look busy managing our little life and tiny home while doing nada to find himself a job. I let him know about that, too. It was not in my Country-Club-Life Plan to be the breadwinner of the family and my husband to look like I just dragged him in off the street!

The last straw for him was turning a whole load of white clothes yellow from the stupid-ugly parachute pants he bought on our honeymoon that had CANCUN in big giant letters all down one leg. When I came home from work and witnessed what he'd done, I started laughing and joking with him about ruining the pants that I loved so much. He flew off the handle at me, so I punched him. *I know, right? How stupid! He's four times my size and could flatten me in two seconds.* That just sent him through the roof! He grabbed me by the neck and began shoving me backwards across the living room into a wicker loveseat that fortunately tipped over, forcing him to let me go. We grappled our way up off the floor, straightening our clothes.

Then we just stood, staring at each other right in the eyeballs, in disbelief, and I muttered despairingly, "OMG, we have become our parents." In my mind I heard these words, "We're not going to be allowed in a country club like this. We've got to straighten up our act!"

However, we couldn't get our act together. We'd crossed a line of trust, fear had settled in, and it spiraled us into this brainless, provoking of one another, and me daring him to hit me. *Good Lord! What was I thinking?* I felt like this switch would get flipped on inside me and I would spin out of control.

When the spin-out was over, we would just go silent a
nd stare at each other with expressions that said,
"Who are you? How did we get here?"

Instead of trying to figure it out, we just got busy. He started some book business, along with a couple of multi-level marketing gigs, that kept him running to meetings all the time. I took on more responsibilities with the adoption agency. Our lack of connection was keeping the peace, but it was creating more and more distance between us. We didn't speak to each other at home. We turned on the charm around our friends and at church so no one would know that everything wasn't perfect with the newlyweds. I knew how to fake like a pro. I was born and raised to hide behind a mask. So, I kept my hopes up that we could attain the Country Club Life, if we just plaster happy faces on after a couple of drinks, just like everybody else and pretend to be the perfect Country Club Couple. The Tulsa Country Club was big and glamorous and just down the highway. I just needed to make Phillip perfectly happy, get him making money again, and for heaven's sake, get him out of those stay-at-home-husband clothes and looking good again!

However, Phillip was not content or happy at all with his multiple money-making gimmicks and the emotional heaviness of my job was weighing hard on me. Discontent and stress were mounting under the swell of tension, brewing the perfect storm. The storm hit our little apartment one Saturday, late morning, just like the weatherman predicted, and I will never forget the aftermath. Phillip was out working his book route, while I was at home cleaning house and jamming out to Janet Jackson.

While singing and dancing with my vacuum, Phillip came storming into the house, got right up into my face, and yelled, "What is this playing in my house!?!"

I was too shocked to respond.

He proceeded to yell again, "I won't have this trash in my house!"

He stomped over to the cassette player, yanked out the tape, unraveled it, and threw it across the room. He stormed back out of the house and slammed the door, knocking all the pictures off the wall in the entryway, shattering the glass all over the floor.

I vividly recall that heart-racing feeling I had experienced so many times as a young girl, after a family feud had just ended and everything went silent as you surveyed the damage.

Then these gut-wrenching thoughts passed through my mind, "I have made a huge mistake. I should have never married this guy. He is not who I thought he was. He makes me feel just like I did growing up."

Then I went into our bedroom, sat down on the corner of our bed, and started beating myself in the head, pulling my hair, and screaming at myself, "How could you have been so stupid! How could you have been so stupid to think that you could ever be happy!" In my mind I heard another voice mocking me with, "You're doomed to be just like your parents! You will never darken the doors of a Country Club!"

**Then boom, just like that,
the enemy saw an opportunity to flood my soul with lies,
and he took it, just like a seasoned opportunist.**

What I didn't know was that Phillip had just the gotten news that his Godfather, Mr. Wilson in Virginia, was in the hospital in severe condition. He flew out the next day to be with Wilson. Within four days, Phillip called with the devastating news that Mr. Wilson had passed away. He sounded like he was having a complete breakdown.

All I could think was, "I've gotta get to my man! He needs me!"

So, I threw together a suitcase, jumped in the car, and took off to Virginia without even notifying my boss. I drove fourteen hours straight through to Mr. Wilson's house, walked in, and found Phillip sitting on the floor of that big, beautiful, now bleakly empty southern plantation home. I ran to him. We embraced. This was the deepest kind of connection I'd ever allowed myself to experience. The kind that only comes from allowing yourself to be completely vulnerable and love hard.

It's amazing how moments of passion can speak more than words could ever say.

When we returned to Tulsa, we had turned a corner in our relationship. We had bonded in a deep way over the loss of Mr. Wilson and reignited our passion for our dreams together. We knew that we could not return to the crazy cycle we had been in and expect to move forward with our dreams. So, we sought counseling for a year from the marriage counselor at our church. What we learned in that year was very impacting and has stuck with me to this day. Within a few months, we were managing ourselves and our marriage better.

However, we were not managing our money so well. Phillip was still floundering around trying to make one of those multilevel marketing businesses work. Poor guy was trying so hard to find some quick money-making gig because he could not find a job in his field of counseling. His floundering caused me to get really uneasy about our future. Then, one day, the sky's opened and dropped a small inheritance out of the sky from Mr. Wilson's death.

Phillip soon began talking about investing and using all this business lingo that I'd never heard come out of his mouth before.

Remember, I did not marry a business guy, I married a preacher man. He was looking for a very lucrative business that required very little overhead. I was quite impressed at first and it raised my eyebrows at the idea of maybe landing our country club membership soon. Within just a couple of days, he came home raving about a brilliant business proposal that he'd just received. Guess what it was y'all? Tanning salons! Yep. Of all the businesses on the planet, he picks tanning salons! I couldn't believe my ears. However, he was so enthusiastic and proud of himself, that I did not have the heart to deflate his big idea with my shock and chagrin.

Before I knew it, he'd found himself a business partner. It was the brilliant fella that put the ridiculous tanning salon investment idea in Phillip's head in the first place and together they opened a brand-spanking, new tanning salon. Everything about it was so humiliating for me. I did not want a living soul to know we were the owners of what I thought was such a cheesy business. If that wasn't bad enough, Phillip's business partner was this little, nerdy guy from college that wore these bug-eyed glasses and used to check me out when we were in college together. *Uuuggghhh! Is this really happening?*

Then, heaven only knows how they were actually able to pull this off, but they found another poor soul and suckered him into investing in the salon. Then those three stooges decided to open two more tanning salons, but not just any ole' salons, they invented Suntan Supercenters! It was like Walmart for hard-core tanners, with blue-light specials and all. For real! This was about all my withering self-image could stand.

Then came the final blow. Phillip came to me confessing that the salons were not making any money and he and his partner were desperate for help. Well, I have to say, I wasn't surprised, as neither one of them knew jack squat about running their own business. They weren't even working in the salons or putting themselves on the schedule. They just hired all these cute little, half-baked chicks with goggle lines around there eyes. You know, like that funny gal running the tanning salon in *Christmas with the Krank's*. If you haven't seen that one, put it on your Must-See List. It's hilarious!

Anyway, they needed someone with business savvy, someone with business experience; maybe even a business degree. That person happened to be me. To save us from financial ruin, it was Darlena to the rescue, just like I did in my family. I was the golden child that made everything better. So, I quit my job and began to manage tanning supercenters! Exactly what my parents had spent thousands of dollars educating me to do. Yay, for me!

The first goal of my business take-over was to get rid of Phillip's partner. It didn't take me long to find out that he was sexually harassing our cute, overly tanned employees, flirting with customers, following them into their tanning rooms, and taking cash from the registers. The day I walked into our office to find him looking at porn on our business computer, he was out of there!

Honestly, as sarcastic as I am being, and as much as those tanning salons embarrassed me at first, I was thankful to be relieved of my job with the adoption agency. It had become so beyond stressful that I'd had an emotional breakdown. No sooner did I come off an emotional crash, I walked straight into a three-car (salon) pile-up! Come hell or high-water, this little tough cookie was going to rescue her husband. He had become so stressed at this point, that he was hitting the local bar before heading home every night. When I couldn't find him (back before cell phones), I could go down the street, open the door to this little bar, and there he'd be sitting with his high-collared, puffy coat on and his hand gripping a glass of beer like his life depended on it. This was not okay with me on any level. I was going to be the heroine of this story and make everything better.

I did make things better. I had those salons running like smooth-sailing ships, but it about cost me my health. I was getting very little sleep as the salons were open for 24 hours. I was eating junk three times a day, as the main salon was enclosed by a wall of fast-food restaurants that I frequented anytime I stopped long enough to notice I hadn't had anything to eat. I was drinking lots of caffeine to keep myself in the game. After about a year of this pace, came the collision. We now had another crisis on our hands—a physical health crisis.

Not only was my body suffering, we also couldn't get pregnant. My lady doctor said she believed it was because my body was under too much stress. Looking back, it doesn't take rocket science to see that, but I was running so hard and fast, I couldn't see the obvious right in front of me. Something had to give.

If there's one thing Phillip and I can claim that we've excelled at in sustaining our marriage, it's managing crisis well.

Some of the things that would have inevitably sent other couple's reeling, cause them to question their marriage, or throw in the towel, we have used to help build resiliency, make us better, and bounce back stronger.

My health crisis, Phillip finding comfort from a bar, and our inability to get pregnant was shouting at us to bring this season of our lives to a halt and get back to being and doing what God had called us to do. So, we began to pray earnestly that the Lord would help us get out of our business obligations and get on with our lives.

Within just a short time, we found a buyer for the salons and our church called and offered us both perfect positions—Phillip, the Dean of the School of Ministry and me, the Overseer of the newly built Maturity Home. We felt peace settle back into our lives like an old friend and I became pregnant within three months. In a sigh of relief, we closed the chapter on the Tanning Salon Years. They were full of hard lessons learned and ended up being shameful for both of us—years we wanted to put far behind us. So, we took a vow of silence to never bring them up again and started a new chapter about building the perfect family.

Phillip

This was a tough transition for me. I knew we didn't belong in Chicago, but the thought of not being a big shot on staff at a church scared me. I hated feeling like a nobody. The stress of being a new-lywed and unemployed wrecked my manhood. Figuring out how to provide for us and how to live out my passion to be a world-changer wasn't working out.

Maybe the reason things didn't work out on my first ministry assignment was that I had married a rebellious woman. That's what some of the leaders at the mega-church told me. I started to think the reason I felt like a failure was because my new bride was not spiritu-ally mature. She wasn't disciplined like me. She didn't pray like me.

Fantasy collided with reality and reality won. Marriage was sup-posed to be about feeling important. My career was not getting off to the momentous start that I expected. The knee jerk reaction to handle my feelings of inadequacy was to put the blame on my wife. That woman God gave me was responsible for everything going bad.

If she would have tried harder and been more spiritual when we lived in Chicago, then I would have been more successful.

Now, what are we going to do? I thought. *It can't be my fault. I was never wrong. I was the mature dedicated one. She was wasting her days watching TV and making little to no contribution to efforts to be an important somebody.*

I was in a deep rational battle. Blaming my wife seemed like the reasonable thing to do. It hit me like a bullet piercing my chest. This woman tricked me. Yesterday, I couldn't imagine life without her and now I couldn't face it with her.

I tried to get spiritual. I looked to the Bible for answers. Adam blamed Eve. I found the evidence in Genesis 3. She was deceived by the serpent and manipulated Adam. She was the first one to disobey God. Adam was coerced by this woman's supernatural mesmerizing powers. Adam was not at fault. He was led astray trying to protect his wife.

I desperately wanted an excuse to blame my wife and my perception twisted my understanding of the scriptures. I manipulated the scriptures to validate my flawed conclusion. The lie was a total rationalization, but it brought me a weird sense of comfort. If it's not my fault, then I don't have to change.

I was blind to how I was showing up, but I was certain that the reason for our fallout was all my wife's fault. My wife's weaknesses were out in the open, but my shortcomings were neatly tucked under many layers of fig leaves. I was disillusioned about the true source of our struggles. I wasn't going to be strapped to this mad woman who could without provocation or justification disrespect me and thus rebel against God. No one was going to disrespect me and get away with it.

The fantasy wife was now this woman God forced on me. To be honest, I wasn't only blaming my wife, I was blaming God for giving her to me. Yes, I had to audacity to accuse God of making a mistake. My pride was leading the charge and I felt very justified in my defensive stance.

Self-righteousness cloaked in doing the right thing was my strategy. I had to force Darlena to walk the righteous path which was about making her more disciplined and more respectful. I can remember doing stupid stuff like criticizing the music she listened to, the junk food she ate, and her endless need to have fun. I was too holy for these activities. Bible-bullets were my favorite weapon. That's a technique self-righteous people use to shame others. I took her struggles and lack of will power and I quoted Bible verses that highlighted those sins hoping that feeling shamed would encourage her to change. That was so wrong. Admitting this makes me feel sick.

I thought to myself, *I will prove that I am right. Being right would give me the upper hand. If she is not going to submit to me then I will withhold my love and affection from her. Let's see how she feels after I ignore her for three days.*

This wasn't God's plan. God didn't blame the woman for the fall of man. Adam was not a victim. Pride and insecurity prevented me from admitting I was wrong. The half-brain idea to reject my wife to get her to respect me was silly. However, that woman I pledged to love a short time ago until death do us part needed correction. Her biblical role was to submit to her husband and do what I said. I believed she was not submitting because she wanted to be in control. This was her way of taking over.

She's doing this on purpose. I had it all figured out. She spent her childhood years planning and plotting to take over my life. The little wounded boy inside of me wasn't going to put up with this rebellious woman. I pulled away from her and decided to armor up.

When she walked into the room and tried to interact with me, I acted like a rejected teenager. I gave her the face. You know, the face that sends a non-verbal message of I don't care, but deep down inside I desperately wanted her attention. I did the opposite when she tried to connect. I turned away if she tried to touch me and walked away when she was talking to me. Typically, she tried to be gentle at first, but if I stayed shut down then she let it rip. The way she talked to me reminded me of how my father spoke to me. He would explode and beat you with his fists and somehow it was all your fault. He got away with it because he was bigger than me, but I was not going to let her emotional rants go unpunished. She didn't hit me with her fists, she stuck a sword into my heart with her tongue. This was intolerable. I couldn't believe she was this immature.

Ignoring her made things worse, but the rejection wasn't the worst decision I made in our marriage. Judging her was the worst mistake. Please understand, it was not just a big mistake, it was a very bad decision. Mistakes are mindless, this was a malicious decision. I didn't simply ignore her. I judged her. I labeled her for being emotionally irresponsible. She was an out-of-control disrespectful, controlling, little woman on the hunt for someone to beat up with her mouth. That judgment created a bulletproof vest around my heart. There was no love getting out or getting in.

My G-rated Disney classic had become an R-rated horror show. It was her plan to lure me into the relationship with her bubbly person-ality and hot body only to capture me and turn me into her web of emotional manipulation. I was reliving my oppressive childhood all over again. These words sound extreme, but they were real thoughts that dominated my boy-man ideas of marriage twenty-six years ago.

I listened to that little voice of accusation on my shoulder that was saying, "She's just like your dad. He wanted to destroy you and so does she. She is going to keep hurting you until you give up. She wants to be in control, she has to be in control, and she will stop at nothing until she has complete control. She wants to be the man in the marriage! You married the wrong person. Run, run, run."

Those voices weren't from God and they didn't reflect the truth. I reduced my reality to misery enforced by my self-pity. This woman that God gave me was doing the opposite of what she was supposed to be doing. Her purpose was to make me feel like a man not to castrate me.

How did this happen? Did I make the biggest mistake of my life? Did I miss God's plan for me? I blamed God for not warning me about her emotional instability. I did all the right things and God let me down. I went to the right college to become a pastor. I went to work for the right church, and I married the right girl. What happened? God should have screened her eligibility to be a worthy spouse for me. How is God going to fix this mess?

Darlena was right. We could have awful arguments and all-out-verbal-wars, but when a crisis hit, we knew how to rally for one another. Wilson's death was a difficult loss. Losing him caused the certainty of my foundation to crumble. I lost my anchor, my rock. He was the one person I could call who would always be there for me. I depended on him to help me make the most important decisions in life.

How was I going to find my way without a captain to guide my ship? Finding a secure path was many attempts to prove my worthiness. I'm embarrassed to admit the schemes that I impulsively created trying to get rich quick. My search for significance hatched several stupid business ideas that crashed and burned.

I must say that Darlena stood by me during that season. Her fierce anger could indeed be converted into crazy love. She was my number one cheerleader. There was no lack of effort on her part to support me. However, her best efforts were never enough to lift the unworthiness that ruled my self-image.

Summary

The first couple of years were rocky because we allowed our circumstances to control our relationship. When things were good, we enjoyed each other, but when things were bad, we attacked one another. We gained powerful insight from our counselor about our quick escalations and giving ourselves to such outrageously, immature behavior. Because we grew up in such volatile and unpredictable environments, we had no grid for living in peace and trust. So, we recreated what was familiar to us by provoking one another to anger and daring each other to escalate.

Our counselor had us practice an exercise that helped us find a breakthrough. He had us find pictures of each other as little kids and carry them with us everywhere we went, sitting them out so they would stay in sight and be looked at frequently throughout each day. He told us to see each other as a tender, innocent little boy and girl, because that's how Jesus sees us, and it would change the way we treated each other. It worked.

Another challenge he had for us that helped simmer down the fighting. He had us ponder this thought: if we fought to win, then that made the other a loser.

Then he posed this question, "Did we ever want the other to feel like a loser?"

The answer was, "No."

I'm so thankful that receiving counsel helped bring awareness. The escalations we were unconscious instigations in our new marriage. The fresh insight helped us bring the curtain down on that crazy provoking-one-another-to-wrath-on-purpose phase before one of us got seriously injured.

Finally, the enemy had scouted out the outer banks of our marriages looking for unguarded entry points to rush in close to where we were most vulnerable with a goal to divide and conquer by planting lies like, "I made a mistake or I must have married the wrong person." He came with one goal in mind, to ultimately destroy our marriages.

One of the weapons the enemy gives us is to twist scripture to use against one another. Self-righteousness and judgment ultimately divided us, making one the winner and the other the loser. For us, the goal was to use being right as a method of manipulation not to support growth. But, if one person is right and the other is wrong, then what has really been gained?

As you read our story, did you see yourself manipulating one another instead of encouraging growth?

Have you ever felt like you married the wrong person?

How did you react to this feeling?

Chapter 5

THE BLAME GAME PLAY-OFFS

Darlena

Having children adds so many new dimensions to a marriage. They can also cause our emotional pendulums to swing from the wildest joy we've ever had to erupt from our hearts to the opposite extreme—the most ferocious fear to ever emerge from the depths of our soul. These emotions can happen within moments of each other and may sound like, "Oh my gosh, I never knew I could love someone so much!" to "Dear God, what if something ever happened to you!" Some couples think that having children will make everything better if their marriage isn't all they'd hoped. However, having children does very little to improve your relationship. Quite frankly, if your marriage is limping along, having children can cut it off at the knees! It is a myth that having kids will fix a broken marriage or help keep "them" around.

Not only can children cause the greatest/deepest emotions we've ever known to erupt/emerge from our guts, they can also cause us to undergo the

most daunting mental, emotional, and physical exhaustion ever known to mankind.

I can only speak from a female perspective. I shall begin with the endearing childbirth experience, which for me was a living hell! We read that *Supernatural Childbirth* book, we got a midwife, we wrote out this perfectly peaceful birth plan, we read books to the baby, and played Beethoven to my belly at night. We fully believed we would bring our angel-baby into the world in a blissful, beautiful way. However, our first child took thirty-three hours to come out of me!

About hour eighteen, Phillip leaned over to ask me ever so gently, "Honey, can I get you anything?"

I grabbed that man by the collar and yelled, "Yes! You can get me every kind of pain killer this hospital has got! And do it NOOOOWWWW!"

After all that, baby girl popped out looking just like her daddy! My panties were in a wad for quite a few months, maybe even years, over that. Oh, and, I threw that dang *Supernatural Childbirth* in the trash!

I'm not going to go into the birthing stories for our next three children, but the other three labor stories were not much different. Three of our babies spent the first few days of their lives in the NICU. Honestly, I don't know how I ever had another one, when after each one I said, "I'm never doing that again!" Still to this day, I will straight up tell you that if I ever hear a women talk about what a wonderfully easy labor and delivery she had (you know the ones that say that their baby just slid right out and she never even knew she was in labor), I envision myself climbing her like a tree and throat-chopping her! My experience was anything but wonderfully easy! Even so, I wouldn't trade my four beautifully unique children for anything in this world.

However, I can say I would not want to go through all that labor, again, to get them here. *Don't tell my kids I said that though!*

My point is having children can be insanely exhausting. So much so, that after all that hard labor and nursing about every three hours during the first 8-12 weeks, I seriously don't remember a thing about my life until I got a decent night's sleep. I only remember feeling like a milk cow. My mom, God love her, spent six weeks with me after each baby. She would come to wake me up in my bedroom when it was time to "milk".

Having said that, I rest my case. Having children takes a toll on a marriage. It took a toll on ours for certain! Do you think that any part of me was thinking about wanting to be intimate with Phillip or have sex? NO! I did not want him to even touch me. All I could think to talk about in my delirium for almost three months was how sleep deprived I was, so I am positive that I did not make for good company. I was totally self-absorbed in all that was going on with me physically, just trying to make it through the waking-up-during-the-night nursing stage and managing my home at the same time.

Watching my mom back down the drive and leave me alone to nurse, change diapers, do laundry, cook meals, keep the house clean, care for all the baby's needs, and try to take care of myself brought on a feeling of despair. I could hear the words to *The Despair Song* from the old T.V. show, *Hee Haw,* playing in the background as I waved bye to her, "Gloom, despair, and agony on me..."

So, back to the marriage. I wasn't thinking about my connection with Phillip in the midst of my despair or how to maintain our intimacy in the thick of the gloom. I wasn't even thinking about how he was doing or what he was doing. All that was going through my mind now was how to lure him into helping me. Maybe if I acted pitiful enough, he would do the dishes or bathe the baby. To his credit, he did help more with the babies after I stopped nursing because then he could feed them with a bottle without me. I have the funniest story about the first time I ever left him with our oldest, Andelyn, while she was still nursing. I went out to just have a little "me time" and do a little shopping. I promised I'd be back for the next feeding but pumped a bottle to leave him just in case. I used a wrap-around nursing pillow that strapped on called, "My Breastfriend." I know, right? When I got back, on time I might add, he had that nursing pillow strapped on with the bottle propped under his arm, trying to create a mock nursing breast. Andelyn was screaming and crying and wasn't having it. He had the funniest look of desperation on his face that I'll never forget. I think I laughed until I peed a little, but Phillip wasn't cracking a smile at the time. Although, it's a funny story he loves to tell now. Come to find out, she had colic and scream-cried like this for what seemed weeks!

> **Yep, having kids affects your marriage. It can cause the atmosphere of your home to be high-octane tense when screaming babies can't be comforted. If you don't handle the tension well, it can cause you to start taking it out on each other. Yeah, we did that.**

Having children can also unleash things inside of you that you did not know you were capable of, good and bad, like a protective kind of love that you've only seen in movies or an insane rage that maybe you've gotten a glimpse of if your favorite superhero is The Hulk. I remember the day that I went Hulk on Phillip the first time. Andelyn was about six months old, we were living in the maternity home, and we were walking out of the church. I don't recall what triggered me, but I had to excuse myself after we were back at the home to take a breather on the front porch.

As I stood there trying to gather myself, I thought to myself, "Oh, God! I've turned into my dad."

I also recall having the sinking feeling that things were going to get worse before they got better. As time went on, I tried to hide the rage inside of me from everyone, particularly Phillip. I could have been acting like Cruella Deville all day at home with the kids, hear his car pull up in the driveway, and snap into my Mary Poppins act. As weird as it may sound, the transformation was so quick that it almost felt otherworldly, like there was another person that lived on the inside of me who threw up a disguise on cue. I freaked myself out a little.

Baby number two added another level of stress and tension, as I had severe back problems while pregnant with her. My lower back spasmed and stayed that way for several weeks, causing me to not be able to stand up straight or pick up Andelyn. I have the gift of ingenuity that's helped me navigate problems well throughout my life. I used it to figure out how to get me and her around the house. I was scooting in a rolling office chair and I taught Andelyn how to climb in and out of her walker by herself so I could also push her around with me.

However, I didn't get much help or sympathy from Phillip during this time. Here's my version as it was etched in my brain. It's a moment that I have never forgotten, and I didn't let him forget it either, for years.

**It was one of those flash experiences that I call,
"Moments of Impact,"
when something happens in an instant that changes you forever
and things are never the same, for better or for worse.**

This particular moment took place the morning I woke up, got out of bed like usual, but couldn't stand up. I was panicked and trying to make my way through the house with thoughts of what could possibly be wrong with me mixed with how I was going to manage a one-and-a-half-year-old like this. This fixer in me concluded that if I could just get to my chiropractor, he could pop me back into shape and I'd be back to myself in no time. I would only need Phillip to drive me.

So, as he was rushing through the living room to head out the door in his important-looking I'm-the-Dean-of-the-School-of-Ministry suit, acting like what was going on with me did not even phase him and basically pretending he didn't even see me, I asked him if he could please take me to the chiropractor. While standing behind the couch, still in my pajamas, holding onto the back of it to support myself—a memory etched in my subconscious—he returned this fly-by response that caused my heart to sink into my gut, "I do not have time for this. I have got to get to work. You are going to have to figure it out yourself." That basically meant, I just needed to pull myself up by my bootstraps and deal with it, cause he ain't got time for it.

He never even paused to look at me with any sort of compassion, he just flew out the door in a flash, sped out the driveway, and I was alone to figure it out for myself. I think I must have stood there in that spot, holding onto the back of the couch in disbelief for what seemed like an eternity. It was like time stopped, allowing me to feel every stinging, painful emotion—rejection, abandonment, aloneness, and fear—making their way slowly through my soul like hot tar, until they reached a dead-end and there they hardened. The most dangerous emotion that I let ooze into my soul in that moment was resentment. I felt my affection for Phillip and any admiration I had for him turn into disdain in an instant and vowed that he would never make me feel that way again. I pushed him far away from me in my heart and decided to practice distance from that moment on to ensure my protection from him.

**There were lots of things lying in waiting
to fill the distance between us,
planted by the enemy to insure our complete separation.**

We did not talk about that moment for a long time. It was like our relationship became a Who-Can-Need-Each-Other-The-Least competition. We started taking on things to do with our time, in what seemed like an effort to out-do one another. I remember one night, I felt like he was winning the Achievement Award and I was just a pawn in his game of success. I was pregnant with our second child, Lydia, and was standing in our kitchen, dressed in overalls, where I had been cooking dinner. (This is the scene he talks about in his version.)

I had to cook special meals for him because he had started a body-building program and entered himself in a 90-day body transformation competition. He walked in the back door, did not even speak to me or Andelyn, who was sitting in her highchair, as he passed through the kitchen to grab his plate of specially made, plain chicken and rice. He went up to the office to eat while he checked in with his online classes for the doctoral degree that he was also working on. When he was done in the office and changed into his workout clothes, he passed back through the kitchen, dropping off his empty plate, still not speaking, and went straight down into the basement to workout with these stupid weights that he had made from empty bleach bottles and sand.

It was official, we had become two ships passing in the night. I felt like I was losing the game and losing my husband as my ship had hit a rocky patch, busting a hole in the side of it. The ship was starting to fill with water. I knew it wouldn't be long before I would sink.

I couldn't keep up the act after having our second baby girl, Lydia. When she was around six months old, I began battling severe postpartum depression. It became so bad, I had thoughts of ending it all. When the thoughts came, they typically sounded like this, "Next time you are driving alone in the car, you should just swerve over into oncoming traffic in front of a semi and end it all." I frequently went to Target at night after Phillip got home and the babies went to sleep, to just get out of the house. Phillip knew what I struggled with mentally, so he feared that I wouldn't make it home from my nightly Target get-aways. Those thoughts are terrible, I know, and I'm ashamed that I had them. I couldn't imagine anything worse, until one afternoon, when I thought the unimaginable!

This was the setting when it happened. Andelyn was sitting on the floor looking up at the T.V. watching the Disney movie, Anastasia, and I was sitting on the couch behind her, nursing Lydia. My head was bobbing, and I was in that drowsy-trying-to-stay awake state, while halfway watching the movie. As I stared lethargically at the T.V. screen watching Rasputin, the evil villain, chasing Anastasia. He started angrily yelling threats, but I heard another voice take over in my head. Instead of the hearing the real words Rasputin was growling as he stood over Anastasia with drool dripping from his snarled lips and threatening to kill her, these were the eerie words I heard, "The next time you think about pulling out in front of a semi to end it all, you should take your girls with you, so you can spare them of ever having to feel the way you do right now."

Oh, my God! Did I just hear what I think I heard? I was startled awake by the shock of those horrific words and this scene of a horror movie that I just starred in. With the sound of the demonic voice with which I'd heard it and the heaviness of death that I felt surge in the room, I was so freaked out that I jumped immediately off the couch, baby in tow and ran to the nearest phone hanging on the kitchen wall. After explaining to Phillip the psycho thing that just happened, he pulled some strings and got me an appointment with a psychiatrist for the very next day, who put me on an anti-depressant. It was the first time in my life that I'd ever been on psychotropic medication and the first time in my life that I ever neglected myself and my kids. Those meds worked, I guess, because they took me from frantically-obsessive to I-don't-give-a-care. I managed to get the girls and I taken care of and to church the first two weeks I was on it. However, by week three, I'd stopped bathing myself and my girls or changing our clothes. I think we stayed in the same clothes for about five days. I'd never not cared about what I looked like in my whole life. I was so checked out that I couldn't pull it together to keep the perfect act going.

Phillip just stared at me, like he was completely wigged out by my behavior and didn't know what to do with me. What was happening to me? This was a nightmare! "I don't give a lick what I look like and my husband thinks I'm a freak!" What could be worse? I couldn't live like this, so after about a month, I got off that stuff. What happened once I got off of it was crazy! The after-effects of that medication ended up having the results of a wonder drug! Whatever that was I took sure did the trick because I was better than before! It was as if I had been living under a dark cloud, then suddenly, the clouds parted and I could see and feel the sun shining again!

Because I went through this horrific experience, I have a deep compassion for people who struggle with tormenting depression. Around the same time that I "heard a voice" tell me to do something unthinkable to my babies, there was a mother somewhere in the United States on trial for drowning her children. I believe this mother had a similar experience to mine, except she didn't have that moment of sanitary to call for help before she followed through with what she heard in her head. She probably didn't know Jesus either.

I'm so thankful I serve a living God who showed up in my darkest moment and gave me the strength to save myself and my baby girls of something potentially life-threatening.

So, Phillip and I may have gotten through that mess and I may have gotten better, but our relationship didn't get any better. We continued to practice distance at home, while faking it at church. Sadly, we even went through the holidays in this condition. If we only knew back them the time and memories, we were wasting. I remember decorating the house that year for Christmas all by myself; putting ornaments on the tree with tears streaming down my cheeks while Phillip sat on the couch watching football. The resentment was rising to a scary level. We didn't even want to be behind a camera together, so that year's Christmas Photo/Card only had our two adorable little girls in it, dressed in the cutest Christmas dresses. Oh my gosh, did I ever have fun dressing little cuties! You know things have gotten bad when you don't even want to be in the Christmas picture together.

I even rang in the New Year alone while he was asleep on the couch. He couldn't even stay awake to turn the page of the calendar with me in hopes of a better year. The needle on my resentment gauge was now reaching the red zone and I could feel that same hatred that I once felt for my dad rising in my throat like vomit you're trying to choke down.

I became obsessed with these thoughts—Why did I marry him? He's doesn't love me. He's only made me feel miserable and stuck at home taking care of kids, just like my parents. One day it hit me, I had become the young girl who told her friend that she couldn't go swimming at the country club. Oh, no! I am trapped once again. This added coal to the raging fire inside of me. I knew something had to change before I suffocated in this marriage that was choking the life out of me or else go crazy from the fear of missing out on the country-club-life that I'd always dreamed of.

Phillip

Having kids was a dream come true. Having kids and taking care of kids were two different experiences, though. I loved the warm and fuzzy moments when our children were wrapped up in a cozy blanket in my arms. They were innocent and quiet. The stress came into the picture with the day-to-day demands of feeding-time, playtime, and sleep time. We weren't prepared for the around the clock requirements of having three kids under the age of five. I never thought trying to create the perfect family would lead to feeling like I was a zombie who worked at a diaper changing factory.

Once again, I reacted to stress by expecting more from my wife. I figured out that living in retreat mode was not going to get me what

I wanted. I launched a more sophisticated approach. I couldn't argue with her and win but I thought maybe I could change her. *That's a great plan,* I thought to myself. *She will thank me after I train her to be a more agreeable person.*

Remember, I was a clinically trained, licensed marriage counselor with a master's degree in marriage and family counseling. I thought to myself, *I will use my counseling tools on my marriage and that will make everything better.*

How do you fix your wife's emotional problems? The right answer is you don't, but I hadn't read that far in the manual. This wasn't an attempt to connect with her. It was my attempt to domesticate her. I tried to defang her fierce womanhood by taking the bite out of her personality. She needed to stop chomping down on me and start being submissive to my God-ordained authority.

Darlena has always been very dedicated to improving herself. She worked out, devoted herself to prayer, and was very conscious about her appearance. If I could persuade her to stop using anger to control me, then she will feel better about herself. Secretly, the real motive was I wanted less conflict in our lives. I deserved a marriage partner who made me feel super important because she followed my lead. I wanted her to have an opinion, but I didn't want her to throw it at me attached to a spear.

I didn't diagnose her and force her into treatment. I tried a subtler, less clinical approach. Modeling change was the answer. I thought if she observed me being respectful then it would inspire her to be the same.

I thought I was doing the right thing by practicing good listening skills and validating her concerns. I made sure that my communication was healthy. I was polite and supportive. Deep in my heart, I felt like I was saving our marriage. However, the root of my efforts was to change her because I hated conflict.

Here's an example of my genius approach to modifying my wife's behavior. I would arrive home after a full day of ministry. The ride home was my time to psyche myself up to be the great man of God when I walked through the door. I would sweep her off her feet with reports of my supernatural work at the church. The real story is there wasn't much sweeping or swooning taking place. There she was in the kitchen, desperately trying to maintain the chaos of raising three toddlers under the age of five. She looked like Lucille Ball doing a cooking experiment that had gone wrong. Our two-year-old was begging for something, there were messes on top of messes, my hot cowgirl wasn't dressed in a sexy cheerleading outfit. She was wearing stained and baggy clothes and the dog was barking. I totally neglected to recognize the obvious needs.

Our exchange started with my super sensitive question, "What are you doing?" (note the sarcasm).

I asked this interrogative question with a pensive look on my face and a big wrinkle in my forehead. You know like your school principal saying, "What are you doing?" when he suspected you were not doing what you should be doing.

She responded, "What do you mean what am I doing?"

The scowl on my forehead revealed the intent of the intervention. My question wasn't an attempt to better understand her, it was my way of calling attention to how she was failing.

My bottom line was, "You suck, it's time to get your act together, woman!"

The internal voice in my head was saying, "You're not doing the right thing because you're not trying hard enough. If you were trying harder, then the house would not be a mess, the kids wouldn't be bouncing off the walls, and that uncooked chicken would be ready for my dinner."

I wasn't helping, I was correcting. I followed her defensive reaction with more interrogation. Shortly after that, she escalated and began to yell at me claiming I was making her feel bad. I was appalled that she raised her voice at me and didn't want my help.

Trying to fix our marriage was a miserable failure. Trying to change her was a bad idea. It didn't work because my goal was off. I wasn't trying to lead or to help my wife, I was controlling her with constant comments about her lack of productivity. She made it clear to me that she felt like she was never good enough no matter how hard she tried. No matter how hard she worked for me, it was never enough. Getting in shape, praying together, cleaning the house, paying the bills, and taking care of the kids was not in any way up to my standards. She was right. My subtle demands were nothing but a list of performance requirements.

I was turning into my dad. The man I swore I would never become like was surfacing in my behavior. I hated when my dad came home and started fussing at my mom about something stupid. He would be away for two weeks and roll through the front door like a prison warden inspecting jail cells. He wasn't looking at the spotless environment, he was trying to find that one spot, that one blemish that was out of order. My dad could make you feel like the scum of the earth. Was I acting like my dad, a heartless demanding ogre?

Truthfully, I was more concerned that our marriage problems made me look bad to fellow pastors and church members. A big part of my fantasy of perfection included me looking like the perfect husband. It was about my image. The great man of God must be able to rule his household. I made sure that when we were at church and in public that my wife toed the line. If I was going to be a respected minister, then we needed to act happy. There was no room for struggle or weakness.

The efforts to change my wife were an attempt to make myself look good and to get my needs met. I needed to be known as the man of the house who was in charge and a great leader in the community. I was pressuring my wife to conform to be like Mary Poppins with her sunny attitude for my benefit. I thought I was serving my godly purpose as a husband. It's amazing how blind I was to the religious spirit that ruled my thinking. I think Jesus called it hypocritical.

Changing her backfired. Darlena was overwhelmed and I thought she wasn't trying hard enough. That was my dad's answer to everything. If something wasn't working, it was because you weren't trying hard enough. The reality was during those formative years of raising toddlers we were both stressed. The problem wasn't effort it was about empathy. It was exhausting during the early years of childhood. Truthfully, I stood over her like a ship captain expecting her to swab the deck with a smile on her face. I hate to admit it, but I had empathy for everyone else but my wife. She needed me to practice caring about her, not expect her to work harder.

I felt strangled by the never-ending conflict. It seemed like we argued about everything. We would start talking about something as simple as who changed the last diaper on one of our three toddlers. Misunderstandings led to escalation which led to accusation. Before you know it, I stormed off to the other room and she chased behind me to get the last word. We would go around and around in circles. She was triggred by feeling unloved and I felt disrespected. She would yell and I would go silent for three days.

Summary

How do you stop the crazy cycle? I felt like I was giving more than my share working on the marriage and she needed to do more. Breaking this pattern seemed impossible. We were very stubborn and entitled to believe that the reason we couldn't get along was the other person's fault. I made a great effort to change my wife by holding her accountable and expecting her to do more.

Instead of communicating our struggles, we just squared off and blamed each other for making the other miserable. We refused to take ownership of our own baggage. In many ways, we were not even aware of how our past was affecting our current reality. Rather, we both just buried ourselves in performing our roles and jobs to perfection in hopes to gain some sense of worth, and maybe if we were lucky, get a little love and affirmation from the other. It just turned into a fighting match and we squared off, again, with aim to win. The thing our counselor attempted to help us with in year one.

Then, you bring kids into the mix and it causes the stress levels of a young couple to rise Starting our family brought on big challenges for us. I totally underestimated how much support Darlena needed from me. I was focused on making my ministry mark in my church career. Young fathers often make the mistake of moving forward without their wives. My career became the focus of all my time, my passion, and my energy. Naturally, my wife got the leftovers. I thought she was being demanding, so I decided to expect change instead of empathizing with her. Changing her was my attempt to reparent her. It was flawed from the beginning. I expected her to pull herself up by the bootstraps and get over it. My speeches about her behavior were rightly received as condemnation, not support. Her fierce independence made it impossible for me to be loving towards her. The lack of empathy for one another drove us apart. She didn't care about my ministry accomplishments and I just wanted her to make me look good. I didn't care about her being worn out from parenting, I just wanted to be affirmed, while she just wanted a lifestyle that I couldn't give her.

What parts of our dysfunctional behavior did you relate to as you read our narrative?

Can you see how you've allowed having children or chasing after a career to negatively affect your marriage?

How have you tried to change your spouse?

What impact did your expectations for change have on your spouse?

Chapter 6

ABDICATION: THROWING IN THE TOWEL

Darlena

E ven though I'd quickly snapped out of depression, Phillip and I were still very much in the same place—living like roommates with benefits and faking happy when we were in public. The only thing we were enjoying together was our cute little girls. He was absorbed in his job, gaining significance from his position as Dean, with his identity rooted in ministry. I was consumed with caring for our little girls, getting my security from being their much-needed mommy, and my identity wrapped around being the CEO of our little home. Except what Phillip did with his life looked so much more impressively important. I was just a mom. I guess it was time, once again, for me to call on my inner Texas Badass Chick for backup. I needed her help to get busy making a life for myself outside of Phillip, if I was going to prove to him that I didn't miss him or need him, and his job was not more important than mine.

I had a best friend back then that also had daughters my girl's ages. We spent a ton of time together during the weekdays while our husbands were at work. If we weren't together, we were talking on the phone, but typically only during the day on weekdays. Well, I started talking to her all the time, even when Phillip was at home, making sure I was standing where he could see me and hear me laughing. This was back before cell phones and I was attached to a wall. If you wanted to be able to walk away from the phone, you had to get these ridiculously long, stretchy phone cords that could reach to the other side of the house! You could easily have yourself all twisted up in it, walking and talking, if you weren't paying attention. When you hung the phone back up, the cord retracted back into a giant, tangled ball that hung down from the phone. I wanted him to see and hear me talking on the phone, to rub in his face in how great a time I was having without him.

My friend and I were always planning and organizing fun play-dates and field trips for our girls. When other moms found out about it, they would want to join us. Eventually, we turned it into like a summer business, allowing other moms and their children to be part of a play date club and attend field trips with us. It was a fun dis-traction for me, kept my girls occupied, and my self-esteem boosted.

As summer was ending, I was offered a part-time job with a design painter. So, I started a babysitting coop to make it possible for me and my friends to trade childcare for free and I could take the job. I loved that painting job so much, that I started my own painting business—painting whimsical children's furniture and room decor. I set up shop in the basement, right next to Phillip's bodybuilding equipment, where we could compete side-by-side and really turn up the heat.

I had things going so well for me that I felt like a super Mom and I didn't need a man for nothin'! My plan to make my life say, "I don't need you!" was in full swing, even to ensure that I was making myself better than Phillip. I had a job, two businesses, was running a babysitting co-op, keeping my house spic-n-span and meals on the table, all while taking darn good care of *our* two little girls. My house was decorated totally cute, like straight out of County Home magazine. I and my girls looked completely adorable from head-to-toe every time we stepped out of the house. Yay, for me, for managing to keep so many plates spinning and still managing to look and feel amazing!

Then I go and attend this personal growth weekend with our pastor's wife, where I discovered that I've basically spent my entire adult life on, "What I could get, instead of what I could give." Wow, this was a mind-blowing revelation that caused deep conviction to rise in me as it related to my marriage. I went home a changed woman. So, noticeably different that Phillip wanted to attend this weekend, as well. He came back repentant and wanting to work on things. But that lasted all of about a month, before we had a blow-up over sex and were squared off in our corners once again.

This was really bad timing, as Mr. Fields was looking quite amazing himself as a result of that transformational bodybuilding program he was committed to. In fact, he was looking dang hot. I tried to not let on that I was staring at him working out when I was painting on the other side of our basement from him. He caught me checking him out once and tried to come onto me, but I refused him. Bad idea. I just hunkered down in my hard-heartedness to ensure he was receiving my strong non-verbal's that I did not care about him or anything he was doing. Even though we didn't speak to each other at home, we faked it when we were at church, in public together, and around people we knew. We were a class act back then. We were so good at our performance, everyone thought we had the perfect little family. Why wouldn't they think that? We looked perfect!

I would have killed before admitting it back then, but I was getting pretty lonely and starved for affection. When the girls were napping, it left opportunity for my mind to wander to happier times when I was having fun and felt adored. My mind started to drift back to my college days at ORU where I had the time of my life. I absolutely loved to dance (still do). My friends and I would go in a big group to a dance club for eighteen and over, take over the dance floor, and jam until we were sopping wet with sweat. I felt so alive when I was dancing and I was quite good at it. I started dating a guy that loved to dance, too, and who was smitten with me. We'd spend hours making up dance moves and routines to wow folks and clear the dance floor on the weekends. Our relationship was full of fun and super sweet.

I started to think about him more and more, until thinking about him turned into an obsession. It seems so lame now, but back then, I had myself convinced that he probably hadn't married because he'd never gotten over me. If I called him, he'd leap with excitement because he'd been waiting for me. I conjured up this ridiculously fantastical idea that we would arrange to meet somewhere in private, run into each other's arms the moment we laid eyes on each other, and begin dancing. He'd throw me back to kiss me and say, "Promise you'll never leave me again."

I'm laughing now, but at the time, it felt so real and so true because that fantasy was fulfilling a deep longing in my soul to be loved and live carefree that was not happening in my marriage. The whole idea deflated the moment I confessed it to my best friend, but what if I hadn't confessed all the ridiculousness going on in my head? What if I had convinced myself to call him? What if he'd responded with a yes? What if….?

I'm pretty certain Mr. Fields had his own fantasies going on, even though our conversations didn't amount to anything, I just somehow knew. Something else I was certain of was that I couldn't take a lifetime of living in this kind of marriage. I desired so much more. I just didn't see myself being able to stay in a marriage where I wasn't enough for my husband—not sexual enough, not spiritual enough, not anything enough for Phillip. I also knew I couldn't endure sharing a life with a man that did not adore me, dote on me like a princess, nor make feel safe and provide for me like a handsome prince should. If something didn't change for us soon to help improve our life together, I needed to have an escape plan in action. Little did I know that big changes were ahead for us, bigger than I could have ever imagined were waiting just around the corner. Maybe my Country Club dream was about to become a reality! After all, the legit, highfalutin Tulsa Country Club was only around the corner and down the hill from our little house.

The change didn't come suddenly, but in a steady progression over a few months. Things were happening behind the scenes at church that would dramatically affect our lives and livelihood; much like an earthquake developing under the ocean floor that would ultimately cause a tsunami. I'll fast-forward the story to the climactic Sunday that forever altered the lives of everyone associated with the church. The head pastor proclaimed from the pulpit during his Sunday morning sermon that he no longer believed the Bible to be inherent, so he was going to write a new theology about inclusion and many ways to God. The staff, as well as the congregation, was dumbfounded, as not one person knew he was going to use his Sunday sermon to make such a claim before the entire church. The following week, a handful of associate pastors, including Phillip, confronted his new theological claims, warning him that they were blasphemous.

The head pastor responded, "If you don't agree with me, then you can leave."

Just like that, Phillip was out of a job. Within a month's time, the mega-church where he had worked and dedicated fifteen years of his life just crumbled. The blasphemy and devastation made the headlines of Tulsa newspaper and headline news, spreading to Christian news media such as CBN and Charisma magazine. High profile Christian leaders were flying in to try to talk sense into our pastor, only to make him dig his heels in further into his newfound beliefs. Even national news media began to carry the story, and news reporters from everywhere began flocking to Tulsa to get an interview with any staff that were willing to talk.

When all the hoopla died down a bit, Phillip began interviewing for a new job with a church or ministry, both in and out of state. Not one church or ministry, large or small, wanted to touch him with a ten-foot pole after they discovered whose church he was from. It was like he'd become tainted because of who he'd worked for—the Blasphemer. It was without a doubt, a case of guilt by association if I'd ever seen one. The reality of the aftermath and consequences on our life left us shocked and chagrined.

Phillip seemed stupefied, like he had no direction for the future. Frankly, it was scaring the crap out of me. I did have compassion for him. After all, his dream job and many long-term relationships attached to it had gone down the tubes. Regardless, how were we supposed to support our family if he couldn't find a job? A job certainly wasn't going to simply fall in his lap while he sat, staring out the window, but without the help of any faith of mine, one did. I'm starting to cringe thinking about telling you about it. A friend of his called with a lead for a (long pause, deep breath, sigh) garbage truck position. Yes, you read right. Oh, for the shame of it! We had sunk to the lowest of low jobs. Do country clubs even allow memberships to garbagemen?

I was too devastated about my reputation and what my friends might think to feel any type of gratitude for the job in the moment. This meant money for our family to eat and keep our house, even if it was garbage money. Never mind that, though, I was peering into the future trying to imagine myself writing our Christmas letter that year—I'm proud to say that even though the mega-church that Phillip has worked for the past fifteen years crashed and burned, he has found employment as a garbage collector. He wasn't even going to be the truck driver, but the guy that jumped out of the truck or hung off the back and emptied the trash into the truck, having to touch it. I thought, *I'll have to burn his work clothes every day! I don't think I can handle this. It's just too much to ask a girl that grew up having money to have to endure. I did not sign up to be married to a trashman!*

After what seemed like an eternity that Phillip worked that loathsome garbage job, spending his spare time staring out the window, expressionless, he had an epiphany. Drumroll please. The words that came of his mouth next felt like boulders falling at my feet, causing a quake that reverberated through my entire body, head to toe.

He said, "I feel like I should start a homeless outreach. I will find God again on the streets, away from the hypocrisy of the church. It worked for Mother Teresa, so it's good enough for me."

What? Homeless outreach? Surely, he was kidding me! I couldn't see for the life of me how we were supposed to support our family with a homeless ministry. But he was as serious as a heart attack because he had that crazed look in his eyes—a man on a mission.

My thoughts were: "This is worse than the garbage job. At least being a trashman brought home a paycheck. Homeless ministers don't make a dime! If we don't get busy making some soon, we're going to be out on the street, living homeless ourselves. They sure as heck don't let homeless people in country clubs!" I wanted someone to shoot me, right there on the spot to put me out of my misery, 'cause I was done with that poverty-stricken, Mother Teresa life and that man who'd drug me into all of it! D.O.N.E.

Phillip

This was the toughest season of our marriage for me. One of the worst things that ever happened to me was the day my dream job ended abruptly. Being a pastor of this mega-ministry made me feel like somebody special. The fantasy of making it to the big-league of the church world caused me to feel like I had arrived. I had my man-card. I was proving my dad's condemning declaration that I would never amount to anything was wrong. I thought I could win his approval by becoming a successful TV preacher. Now that was impossible.

I was knocked off my high horse of self-importance after the church crashed. I plunged into binging behaviors. I knew I couldn't run away because I had a family to take care of. Day after day I faced the impossible task of trying to rescue people who were drowning in the disillusionment of the church war. I wanted to stop all feelings, both good and bad. I could feel my brain start to shut down as I entered my nothing box and sat glued to the TV for hours.

Carb-loaded snacks became my best friends. Nachos stacked high and piled deep with cheese and jalapenos were my favorites. Eating a bag of chips took about as long as an episode of Seinfeld. It got worse when I started drinking. I numbed out weekend after weekend with junk food and a good bottle of wine.

The ugliest habit was my sexual acting out. I reverted to my adolescence. Internet access was a new thing. I spent hours fantasizing about other women as I sat up late at night glued to the computer screen. Pornography was not my escape, but that did not justify my inappropriate lust for fantasy experiences. I coerced my wife into bedroom stuff trying to spice up our intimacy. She became my sex object. I knew she didn't want to be with me which intensified my loneliness. Sex left me empty and us very disconnected.

I could tell Darlena had lost respect for me. I had lost respect for myself. Self-hatred filled my soul. The thought of being a failure in my thirties was a nightmare. Two college degrees, fifteen years of ministry experience, and nothing to show for it. Unimportant and uninvited were stamped across my forehead. Every time I tried to fit myself into a new church or run with a new group, they pushed me out. The rejection I felt was unbearable. Where do I belong?

My concern went from personal embarrassment to trying to figure out how to support my wife and little girls. It's funny how your priorities flip when your world crashes down around you. I was willing to do anything short of something illegal to earn enough money to pay the bills.

I started an outreach to the homeless in our community. The motivation wasn't this Jesus-like-compassion for the lost. The appearance may have been martyr-like, but it wasn't. I was shaking my fist at God because He allowed the church to crash. Plus, hanging out with the down and out made sense because I could be around people who identified with how I felt. I was what my dad told me as a kid, "a piece dirt hanging a worm's butt." In my mind, I belonged with the displaced and dispossessed. Garth Brooks' song about having friends in "low places" bore witness for me: "Well, I guess I was wrong I just don't belong."

By day, I was a want-to-be-martyr to the homeless; by night, I was a numbed out burn out preacher. I hated my life. Time was passing and I was missing out. I needed help, but I was too proud to ask for it. It's funny when I look back at this season of struggle. The men I helped would have been happy to exchange lives with me. Their big regret is how they allowed their addictions to destroy their families, but I couldn't see that I was doing the same thing to my family. I was abundantly blessed with a beautiful dedicated wife and precious little girls, but I couldn't enjoy them.

I was punishing myself. Life on the street and the labor and toil was self-inflicted. I had developed self-hatred as a boy because I wasn't man enough to stand up to my dad and stop his abuse of my mother. Powerlessness convinced me that I was a weakling. The church collapse was a replay of my family dysfunction. The bad guy, the senior pastor, was hurting people and I couldn't stop him. I vowed to myself as a child that I would never be a part of anything as an adult that hurt people. I felt like the captain of the Titanic watching people jump into the icy water. This was all my fault.

Maybe this is as good as it gets. Maybe this is what I deserved. I didn't see a way to turn things around. I felt like giving up. There was no clear path to win my battle with Darlena and I didn't think there is a way to clean up the big church mess. I hid in my cave and resigned to wallow in the mud with my new tribe—The Down and Out. I gave up.

Summary

The church crash broke me. It sadly revealed that my position as a pastor was my identity. The disillusionment was real. The addictions manifested to numb the powerlessness and worthlessness. They became my replacement for the ministry failures. For Darlena, nothing came of that silly fantasy, thankfully, but she shared that story to help make a point. Instead of turning to God and one another, we were turning away to stuff and other people.

Giving up on one another opened a very scary door to bondage. If you allow distance between you, regardless of what caused it, beware. There are lots of other people, places, and things waiting to help you fill that void. Practicing distance in marriage leaves lots of room for other things to fill in that space, widen the gap, or cause you to decide you don't want to repair it because the space fillers and gap dwellers are so much more fulfilling and make you feel so great about yourself—make you fill like a man, compliment your looks, flirt with you, laugh at your jokes—and possibly lead you to the point of no return.

Have you found yourself turning away from each other and God while turning to stuff and other people?

What or who are you turning to in order to find love?

What doors have you opened that could lead you to bondage and widen the gap between you?

Chapter 7

It's Time to Get Real in Order to Heal

Darlena

So, there we were, with a homeless ministry. Yet, my heart was not in it. I felt an apprehension about being involved with the homeless that kept me observing from the sidelines with my girls tucked safely behind me.

However, I do have to credit Phillip for this, when he set his mind to do something, he is passionate about, he doesn't mess around about it. He put together a Board of Directors and rallied a small group of volunteers together. Before I really understood what had transpired, we had donations coming in and volunteers showing up early every Saturday morning to our home to make hundreds of sandwiches. Our family, the volunteers, and the sandwiches would get loaded up in cars, creating a convoy headed for downtown Tulsa, not far from where we lived. We'd drive to a very rough and raunchy area of town, park outside a prostitute/drug house and yell, "Is anyone hungry?" Homeless men and women would start coming out of nowhere and begin crowding around the cars. We had our little girls with us, so the hungry, homeless hoards packing in around us made me pretty nervous.

We began to learn people by name and make conversation with them, which helped my anxiety drop immensely. Eventually, we let the girls stand in the back of a truck and help hand out food—a sweet memory etched in my mind—and the homeless people loved seeing them.

Within a short amount of time, the homeless ministry grew so much that we outgrew our house for the sandwich making. Besides new volunteers joining our outreach crew, we started having entire churches and organizations get involved, which gave us access to a commercial kitchen for preparing food. So, we upgraded from only sandwiches to hot meals, toiletries, and other necessities. One of the organizations sponsored outreach t-shirts, which made the ministry seem like a legit organization that folks were proud to wear the name of on their back.

If you haven't already noticed, I started to change my tune regarding how I felt about us having a homeless outreach. However, I held Phillip to his promise that he'd never bring one of those homeless men to our house. What I eventually learned was, although the outreach didn't bring us much money, it brought us a lot of attention, which I thoroughly enjoyed. People thought we were such a good-hearted and self-less couple and would go on and on about how they admired what we were doing. I secretly relished all the sappy, ego strokes, as they boosted my morale. All the accolades helped take my mind off the nail-biting reality that we had **zero money**! Seriously, we had no money in the bank, we were getting our food from a food bank, and I was on birth control to make certain we didn't get pregnant while we were in this shape.

Somehow, someway, sometimes at the last minute, we would get the money to pay all of our bills. By an act of God, we managed to acquire everything our family needed. By a miracle of God, we also got pregnant in spite of our preventative measures. Thank goodness the Good Lord knows us better than we know ourselves! He knew we needed another baby, during a season that it didn't seem wise to have one—a baby whose name was Joy.

We had no money, so we knew what we had to do help us bring our third little one into the world. Want to guess what that something was? I had to do the unthinkable. Me, all by myself, had to apply for Welfare! I tucked away my diamond wedding ring that Daddy made me, dug out the silver one Phillip bought to shut me up on our honeymoon, sucked up every ounce of pride I had left in me, and drove down to local Department of Human Services and signed up to have a baby for free. Unbeknownst to me, there were all kinds of programs for folks who had no money, so I signed up for everything stuck in front of me—free milk, free diapers, free medicine, and Lord, help me when I say this, food stamps. How humiliating and needfully humbling all at the same time. Thank God.

While I was standing in line awaiting my turn with a social worker, my mind raced back to a time when I was a little girl, shopping with my momma at Piggly Wiggly, standing in the check-out line in our Nieman-Marcus clothes to pay for our cart overloaded with groceries; waiting for the pitifully dressed, white trash folks whose snotty-nosed kids had no shoes on their filthy feet, tear off their food stamps to swap for the little bit of food necessities they had in their cart. Now, here I was standing in those white trash folks' shoes. Oh, how far I had fallen down the social class scale. The view was very different from way down there, like going from powerful to powerless, significant to insignificant, secure to insecure, perfection to imperfection, or more honestly, hopeful to hopeless.

While our two little girls were anxiously awaiting the arrival of their new baby, I was straining to feel happy about bringing another child into our unhappy marriage and financial condition. Phillip, from what I could tell, was busting his butt to build his homeless outreach, which had now zeroed in on men and restoring them back to a dignified life. At this point, he felt that in order to take the ministry to the next level, he needed to realistically know what it would take for a homeless man to get off the street. So, he concocted a brilliant idea. He concluded that if he could live with them for a short while, that he would understand. Shocking! I was literally freaked out by the idea of it. He did it nonetheless.

Momma came to stay with me and the girls. Phillip took with him only a backpack with a Bible and a few necessities, the clothes on his back, a ball cap to help disguise who he was and only few dollars in his pocket. Then, he took off on foot, as we did not live far from downtown, with a goal to live on the streets disguised as a homeless guy for seven days. He promised me he would not sleep on the streets but stay at a residential facility that only charged $5.00/night. It was not much of a step up from the street, but at least it came with a locked door for protection at night while asleep. I know this sounds a little farfetched, but it is a true story, although I still find it hard to believe that he actually did it.

Those were very unnerving days while he was gone, worrying every waking moment if he was okay. He had his cell phone with him, but kept it turned off to save the battery for emergencies. So, a couple of times, I went driving around to see if I could spot him and see with my eyes that he was unharmed. As dreadful as this week was, it undeniably helped me see that I was still very much in love with Phillip, as my heart ached for his safe return. I'd just locked all my feelings away to survive in our shut-down marriage. The worry and the ache made the few days that he'd been gone seem long and drawn out.

Before dawn on his sixth day away, there came a long, loud knocking at the front door. Momma and I both woke with a start and were very hesitant to go near the door.

It was still too dark outside to see anything from the window, so I yelled from across the room at whoever was behind that knock, "Who is it?!"

I could hear a deep, faint, strained voice respond, "It's me."

It was Phillip! I darted for the front door, frantically unlocked and opened it, as Phillip came crashing inside the house and did a faceplant onto the floor. My mom and I dragged him to the couch, where he laid half-conscious while we got his nasty clothes off, which went straight into the trash, I might add. As gross and smelly as he was, I was so relieved to have him home safe and sound, and I let him know it. I just didn't allow myself to get too vulnerably sappy while communicating my sentiments. Fear and distrust kept me guarded. After I got him all cleaned up, he literally did nothing but sleep, eat, and drink water for three days. Then, he seemed to ease back to himself. So, we concluded that he must have just been famished, dehydrated, and deprived of sleep.

Not too long after Phillip recovered from his homeless adventure, I had our third little bundle of joy. I'm surprised the stress of him falling in the door that night didn't throw me into early labor, but she arrived on schedule, perfectly healthy and able to come straight home without a NICU stay, like our first two daughters. While I was in recovery from having our baby, in the throes of sleep deprivation and all night nursing (what I called the milk cow phase), and my mom was back to help around the house, Phillip dove back into working with his board members to ramp up the outreach to accommodate what Phillip had learned from his time on the streets staged as a man trying to regain his life. I wish I had time to share about his experience and what he learned, as it was heart-wrenching, yet very eye-opening. However, I will say, he determined that if he was going to get men off the street and back to being a contributing citizen to society, he had to provide them with a sustainable job, decent income, and adequate housing.

Once our little bundle was sleeping through the night, I was out of the milk cow phase and could handle normal life again, I discovered all that Phillip had been up to. He'd begun a construction site clean-up business. Some board members purchased a dually truck, front-end loader, and other necessary hand tools for such a business. A pastor donated a house for the residential site, which had already been all fixed up and full of men living in it. I also had a job waiting for me. I'd been nominated by the Board to be office administrator of the whole kit and kaboodle. This caused the tension between Phillip and me to mount. It mounted so that there stood a mountain between us—a mountain of disappointment, distrust, unforgiveness, resentment, neglect, and abandonment.

With the addition of the business and residential site, it got to where Phillip was gone from sunrise to sunset, literally, 6:00 a.m. to 9:00 p.m. He was responsible for picking up the men, driving them to the job site, supervising and working alongside them all day, helping them get dinner, and discipling them at night. When he got home, I'd have his dinner waiting. The girls would already be in bed, so he'd get his food, go straight to the living room with it, eat in front of the T.V., and zone out until he fell asleep.

A few weeks of this grueling schedule led him to start drinking at night to wind down. Once he got sloshed, he would get super emotional and want sex, like clockwork. There's nothing I hated worse than sex with a sloppy drunk guy. So, I endured this for only so long, until I started my treks back to Target after the girls were fast asleep, to avoid the sloppy, emotional, drunk sex escapade altogether.

Then, he upped his game. He started coming home from work already sloshed and becoming more and more aggressive as this went on. The night that he slung his plate against the wall because he was disappointed with dinner was the night I said in my head, "I'm done." According to my perception, he had a new love—a homeless ministry—it got the best of him and his time. I couldn't take being the roommate with benefits, who got his leftovers when he got home, anymore. He had this whole other life that neither me nor the girls were a part of. You could say that he was having an affair, but with homeless men. Yep, the competition was high back then! On my nightly, routine drive to Target after the dinner plate incident, I called my momma to confess our situation. I knew that I had to start plotting my get-away plan.

For months after, we just continued to live with more of the same, except Phillip started to get sick. It seemed like every weekend with what seemed like the flu, he'd crash on Friday night, but come Monday he'd seem to be fine and hit the grindstone again. During these weekends, he would just sit in front of the T.V., zoned out, eating and drinking non-stop, while I and the girls went on about our lives. The girls played all around him and he seemed to not even notice them. We even went to church without him.

After weeks of seeing him sit night after night, weekend after weekend in front of the T.V., I could feel my resentment starting to build until it felt like hatred. I blamed him for me not having the county club life that I'd always wanted, not having any friends, and for not having any fun anymore. I wanted the misery to end. I wanted a different life. I wanted the life I'd been fantasizing about since I was a girl. When the time was right, I was going to leave with my little girls to have it.

In my mind, he'd withheld his affection from me for so long, surely by now, he didn't love me anymore, so he wouldn't even care if I left. He didn't deserve for me to continue to stay with him, cooking, cleaning, and doing his bookwork for him. I felt revenge rising. I wanted him to hurt like I'd been hurting. I wanted him to feel all alone in front of that stupid T.V. pounding nachos and drinking boxed wine. I wanted him to realize what he'd been missing out on, day in and day out for days, weeks, months, and now going on years!

Then, finally, s.h.i.t. hit the fan. About a year after our third daughter was born, Phillip got sick one weekend, per usual, but this time, he didn't recover. Come Monday, he couldn't get out of bed. He was burning up with a fever and unable to keep anything down. Without money or medical insurance, we didn't know what to do. On the advice of a chiropractor friend, we went to a doctor that practiced traditional and alternative medicine.

After much testing, he gave us the diagnosis. The doctor's words were like a punch to the gut that slammed me against the office wall with their impact.

"Phillip has Hepatitis-B," he said in what seemed like a deep, monotone voice in slow motion.

He continued before I had even regained my composure, explaining that Phillip's body was racked with it because it had gone untreated for so long. The damage to his liver was now so severe that there was little hope of recovery and could potentially end fatally. The doctor's prognosis slimed me with despair that went oozing all down my head to my feet. It was so heavy and weighed me down so I didn't think I would be able to walk out of the office.

I'll never forget the ride home from the doctor's office that day, in the silence of the shocking news, just staring out the windshield like zombies as I drove slowly and methodically home. My mind raced with hopeless thoughts of how I'd been planning to leave and now I had to stay. Was I going to become a widow with three children to raise on my own? How would I be able to pay our bills and keep our house now? And take care of a deathly ill man and three little girls? All the questions and thoughts made my vision blurred. I settled down by just taking care of the task at hand, which was getting us back home in one piece.

The days and nights seemed to all run together after this, as Phillip never slept. He began treatment but continued to decline. He lived on the couch as he had to stay sitting up. Lots of people came to visit, pray for him, and leave us something to eat or a little money, even the Pastor of our church that had fallen apart visited us. When Phillip didn't get better, people stopped coming by the house. When I was at church, it seemed as though people ran out of things to say, so they just said nothing at all.

Some just stared at me with these pitiful looks that said, "Oh, there's the lady whose husband is dying." Then they would gaze down at my girls as if to say, "Oh, and there are the poor little soon-to-be orphans." Then they would look at each other with a grimace that said, "Let's not get too close, their misfortune might rub off on us." Then there were those who tried not to make eye contact with me at all. I thought, "This is what lepers must have felt like." I was grateful for the people that weren't afraid to come to speak to us or just give us a silent hug. It helped me feel like there was still another human being on the planet and I was not alone in my tragedy, even if they couldn't help me at all.

Phillip continued to lay on the couch and watch Christian T.V. programs one after the other and call every prayer line that popped on the screen.

The despair was becoming too much for me to bear. The Texas badass crumbled into a depression, darker than I had ever known. It seemed suffocating, with ankle weights of hatred, bitterness, and contempt. I was angry with God, mad at the world for my plight, and hated myself for ever allowing myself to get in this situation. I married this man to make my dreams come true, only to have him drag me into a living hell!

I began taking nightly runs to Target again just to get out of the sick house and feel connected to society. I started taking the interstate in hopes that I'd get hit head-on by a semi and put out of my misery. Phillip knew what was going on with me and stayed in fear the entire time I was gone, afraid that I wouldn't make it home.

One night, I drove to the Tulsa Country Club on my way home after it was closed and all dark inside. I sat in the parking lot and stared at it, as I replayed in my mind all the silly dreams that I'd ever had about ever darkening the door of a place like that.

Then, as I was putting my car in gear to drive home, I muttered these words, "This place is not for the likes of me."

I waved goodbye to the country club and all the dreams I had wrapped around it. I went inside my little house, and could hear the T.V. blaring a Christian program, although Phillip was asleep with his head bobbling. I just stared at him a little while.

Then I went in my babies' rooms, stared at them, and listened to them breathe, as I prayed a desperate prayer, "God, if You are real and You can see me down here in this little house and You can hear my small voice, please help me. I can't continue to call myself a child of God and live in this kind of torment. Please end it or take me home, because I'm too chicken to take my own life and I have nowhere else to turn."

I'm not exactly sure how much time passed after my prayer, by not long after, I get a phone call from Mom. She explained that she and Dad were at a three-day conference in Dallas because an acquaintance called and said she was prompted by the Holy Spirit to tell her about it. At that moment, she was buying the conference speaker's book and going to overnight it to Phillip. She believed this book and this man's ministry held some answers for Phillip and would help him. So, we got the book and Phillip read it, and kept reading it over and over. Every time I looked in the living room, it was in front of his face.

After a couple of days, I say to him that I can tell he really liked that book and shared how Mom said that the author had a ministry and retreat that people who had financial challenges could practically attend for free. Then I went about my business and Phillip disappears. Come to find out, he went upstairs to our bedroom/office to sign himself up for the program.

I then ask, "Did you just sign yourself up?"

He admits that he only signed himself up because he didn't think I'd want to go, which makes complete sense, considering our state of being and the fact that I was at odds with God and the church.

However, what came out of my mouth next did not make sense, so it had to have been a divine intervention of God that caused these words to utter from my lips, "Well, if you go by yourself and get healed, only half of you will be healed, because we are one."

Once he recovered from his dumbfounded state, he turned around and went right back upstairs again to sign me up for the ministry program as well.

Little did we know that the ministry was all the way in Georgia and was two-weeks long. But my precious, reliable Momma drove up from Texas to stay with our babies, gave us money to travel with, and off we went on a road trip from Tulsa, Oklahoma to Thomaston, Georgia, a state we'd never been to, a town we'd never heard of, and a ministry we knew little about beyond that book.

We hadn't spoken for at least three days prior to getting in the car together, so the first leg of our trip was filled with hours of awkward silence. Phillip finally broke the ice by thanking me for coming with him, and of course, it made me cry. He's always been great at taking that role when we've been in gridlock. By the time we were mid-way through our trip, we were laughing and enjoying ourselves. Who knows the last time we'd been alone together, much less on a get-a-way?

However, as we crossed over into Georgia, we began to go deeper and deeper into the woods, away from civilization. So, we started to get a little nervous as to what we might be getting ourselves into with this ministry. We think they mentioned something about deliverance and we'd never experienced that before. Also, we had not been this far away from home. So, we made a commitment to each other that if the folks at this ministry pulled something weird, like whipped out snakes or something, we'd just get the heck out of Dodge and have an awesome two-week vacation.

I'm sure I've got you on pins and needles, so I'll relieve you by letting you know that it wasn't weird, no snake-handlers or cult members dancing around a fire. Sorry, if you were amping up for a thriller. However, the outcome was admittedly one of the most thrilling of my life and like nothing I'd ever encountered before. However, it was completely orchestrated by God and very biblical.

The first meeting took place on a Sunday night and was an introduction and overview of the program, as well as a worship service. During the worship, I heard the Lord speak to my spirit, "I heard your cry of desperation. I led you to this place to end your torment. Watch and see what I do for you because of how much I love you." My aching, questioning heart was so moved by these words of hope from a Heavenly Father who saw me and heard me, I could barely see the words to the songs on the screen through the tears that flooded my eyes. I gripped Phillip's cold hand, feeling the same anticipation as that young girl at summer church camp so antsy to get to the altar to experience Jesus, that she could hardly contain herself from barreling down the aisle. A deep faith rose up on the inside of me that God was about to shift my life, now our life, as dramatically as He did after that night.

I sat on the front row in great expectation, posturing myself to receive everything God had for me from every teaching, prayer, and ministry time, with Phillip right beside me. On Tuesday afternoon, we were taught about the spirit of envy and jealousy. During the time of ministry afterwards, the teacher prayed for deliverance from self-hatred attached to the spirit of envy and jealousy to come out. Before he could finish, an entity came screeching out of my chest in a voice I could never imitate even if tried, and with such a force, that it pulled me out of my chair onto the floor in front of my chair. It was a completely other-reality kind of experience, but yet so real.

No one was touching me, waving a wand over me or even near me. Phillip was beside me with his eyes closed and focused on what was going on with him. It wasn't a worked-up atmosphere with anyone yelling a sweat-slinging sermon, chanting incantations, or voodoo dancing. It was a simple, normal-toned prayer, commanding something that wasn't of God on the inside of me to leave in the authority of Jesus' name and whatever that something was, obeyed. I have never questioned what happened to me that day or how it happened. All that has mattered to me was that I could circle the calendar on June 11, 2002, as the last day that I ever experienced suicidal depression. *I told you the story was going to be thrilling. Was I right?*

That's not all, at some point during the program, we're pretty certain it was during what the ministry called, *The Father's Love*, Phillip was miraculously healed of Hepatitis-B! People, you don't get healed of that. According to medical science, once it's in you, it's always in you. But we have documented medical records to prove there are no traces of it in his body anymore. I know it sounds fantastical, like something that only happens in the movies or to other people, but never to you. But it's absolutely true, with no embellishments whatsoever. Scout's honor!

Needless to say, we felt like newlyweds that had been given a new lease on life! Our marriage was restored, years that had been stolen were redeemed, and we looked at the future with great anticipation of never shutting up about what God had done for us! My country club dream had nothing on this, y'all! I mean, I had my husband back, I had my life back, and new lenses to see life through. Those are things to get dang excited about and makes dining at a stuffy country club seem meaningless and empty.

Our story at this point, was more than I ever wanted, wished for, dreamed of, or fantasized about. That all paled in comparison to God giving us the desire of our heart aligned with His will and purpose for our lives. This was a fresh start, a new chapter, and the major turning point of our lives and our marriage.

**It was like the old saying goes,
"We finally got our head screwed on straight."**

Phillip

My quest to make everything that went wrong right forced me into burnout and deep disillusionment with God and the church at large. I was sick of talking about it. Besides, nobody cared, no one was willing to get in the mud with me. I was disconnected from God, my wife, my friends, and myself. All my super spiritual efforts to be a great man of God failed. Failure felt like the end.

The zeal that controlled me turned into rebellion against the god of the self-centered church. I was hell-bent on proving that the narcissistic leadership of the church was wrong. It was about making a statement against the organized church and not about helping people like Jesus did. I don't want to chase that theological rabbit, but my heart was broken over how I'd spent fifteen years building a church and we spent millions of dollars to build a shrine to the puffed-up ego of one man. I needed to do something to make myself feel better about this colossal failure.

I ran myself into the ground. Every opportunity I had to help a lost soul felt like retribution to me. Giving poor people a job, a sandwich, and a place to stay was my way of trying to fix my brokenness. Desperation drove me to work like a slave. I spent my days doing very hard labor. Most of the time we were called upon to clean up trash. Everyone on the job sites looked at me and my guys as no-good bums. I over-identified with these men. Their lives were beyond repair. That's how I felt.

I took on the mentality of a homeless person. Life wasn't fair, everyone was out to get me, and I wasn't going to allow anyone to control me. I needed Darlena to intervene during this time, but she couldn't stop me. She kept trying to go along with me to be my support, but I was possessed with an unrighteous anger. The whole time, I was subconsciously protesting how I was treated and expressing it through self-destruction.

Getting sick rattled me. I knew I was flirting with disaster. The inevitable was unstoppable. The harder I worked the worse I felt. The worse I felt the harder I worked. One day, my body stopped. I couldn't do it anymore. I reached my end and I couldn't go one more inch. Darlena's version of the circumstances that led up my downfall is right on. The only thing I would add is that I felt like a man riding passed a sign warning him that the bridge was out. After seeing the warning sign, I smashed the gas pedal to the floor. I didn't turn back. I wanted something to happen that would bring change. I had no idea how painful the consequences would be that followed. I got everything I wished for.

Dark accusations were flying around in my head. "I deserve this." "I told you so." "You're never going to amount to anything." "You're going to die and leave your children fatherless." "You're a big screwup." "You don't matter." "God is mad at you and you deserve to suffer." I felt like a defenseless wounded animal surrounded by a pack of hyenas.

Everything changes when you come face-to-face with death. It was the ultimate wake-up call. Everything stops. The responsibilities don't matter, my reputation, my opinions, my feelings—nothing mattered. It's was all meaningless in the face of death. I didn't want to argue, I didn't try to get my way. I didn't think about how my wife didn't measure up. I was beyond broken, death was imminent, and I needed to say my goodbyes.

Suffering attracts weird people. Remember the friends of Job in the Bible? These guys felt it was their duty to tell Job why he was suffering. Read the full story. They were called to repentance before the story was over. Pharisaic people say insensitive, critical stuff to people stuck in hardship. I knew they meant well, but it was very degrading for people to be preachy to me. The worst part was the loneliness I felt.

Darlena and I were miles apart when this happened. The distance was the result of years of fighting for control in our relationship. I was hard-headed and stubborn, blaming her for most of our problems, but I realized in that moment that she was the only person in my life who stayed by my side through it all.

Instant humility followed by a rush of terror filled my soul. I was humbled and very scared at the same time. I had no time to be demanding about my situation. "Help me, please someone come to my rescue, deliver me from death," I cried. I needed someone strong enough to look me in my downcast eyes and tell me it was going to be okay.

One day, I was in the bathroom getting ready for a doctor's appointment. I rested my frail frame on the edge of the tub trying to catch my breath. My arm muscles quivered as I sat down.

"I can't do this anymore, Lord, please help me," my desperate prayer took three seconds.

I heard His voice, "I'm going to heal you, son, but it's time for you to get real with me."

That word became a seed of hope. I didn't get healed in an instant, but I knew that God had a plan to heal me.

**The moment I gave up and stopped fighting
God and my wife, healing began.
Surrender was the way forward.**

Summary

It took us almost losing everything before we discovered how blessed we were. Values change when you come face-to-face with death. We realized I didn't want or need the fantasy life. A Disney wife or a country club life had nothing on finding a real abiding connection. We wanted to be together, not because we were perfect for one another, but because we knew how much we needed one another. The goal of our marriage changed. We wanted the real, not the fantasy from that day forward.

Healing can't come in your marriage when you are carrying bitterness toward one another. Change starts with personal repentance and taking full responsibility for your part in the marriage dysfunction.

Are you ready and willing to take full responsibility for your part in your marriage dysfunction?

What are you holding against your spouse?

What do you need to repent of?

Chapter 8

THE RESPITE:
A SEASON OF CRAZY FAITH AND UNCOMMON PEACE

Darlena

So, remember back in Chapter 1, when I let you folks in on a little internal vow I made? If you can't recall, here's another saying to help jog your memory, "Never say never." Like, never say that you will never live in a trailer again! I didn't even say it out loud! It was a silent promise I made in my head. However, despite my secrecy, somebody important up there must've heard me whisper the vow to myself that I would never, in all my born days, live in a white trash, trailer house again, and decided to either use it for my own good or for a really bad joke—I still haven't decided. However, the next decade of my married life was lived out in a house on wheels, nevertheless.

> **Funny how God, in His redeeming power, can take the agonizingly poignant things from our lives that we hate—the unrivaled ugly, detrimental, shameful things—and redeem them into something that we**

fiercely love, find deep joy in, and marks the most endearing moments of our lives.

If that's news to you, it's the best news you'll ever hear. It's my favorite thing about Jesus. One of those redemptive things for me was a trailer house. The one I grew up in contained the most dreadful and traumatic memories of my upbringing. The mobile homes (note this is plural) I lived in during this next season that I'm about to unpack for you, represent a crazy mix of peaceful sweetness, a little adventure, and a lot of faith.

After Phillip and I were healed and delivered, we came up with this wild plan. We stepped outside of our norm and followed through with it after the encouragement of our closest friends. Phillip's doctor strongly recommended he make a complete lifestyle change to fully recover and get his strength back from Hepatitis-B ravaging his body. At the same time, we found out that the South Georgia healing ministry had a campground where you could live for next to nothing if you had your own trailer.

So, we bought this old, hideous and undersized mobile home, called a park mobile (a cross between a travel trailer and mobile home for those of you who don't know your trailers) with one tiny everything—bedroom, bathroom, and so on—for a couple thousand dollars. It was tan, brown, and orange, and to add to the sheer attractiveness of its appearance, it had two big sheets of plywood nailed to the side to protect the sliding glass doors during travel. Then, we bought an old, faded, blue and white Ford pick-up, which we fondly named "Bubba" for a couple hundred bucks. It had an engine powerful enough to haul that beauty of a trailer to the southern hills of Georgia, where we were going to live in bliss at a campground in the valley. I know, you're thinking we were crazy, and you aren't the only ones that thought that. Much to our surprise, we didn't even care. We admittedly were crazy—crazy happy.

Now, I want you to take a minute to get a picture in your mind's eye of what our rig looked like cruising down the highway. We looked like a hillbilly and his trailer trash wife with their three young'uns headed to the Talladega Superspeedway in Alabama for a racing weekend! I didn't know whether to laugh or cry at the sight of us. Thinking back now, I find it mind-boggling how I went from living in complete anxiety over perfect appearances and dreaming of being a card-carrying member of a country club, to looking like the modern-day Beverly Hillbillies, driving to the deep-woods of South Georgia to live at a campground in a shrunken trailer. It was quite a miraculous transformation, I must admit.

Like I said, it was a crazy plan that required a lot of crazy faith and had us looking pretty crazy, too. The reason we didn't care about how we looked was because being joyful and alive and together meant so much more to us at this juncture in our lives than appearances. It was the closest we'd ever come to experiencing freedom, despite how we looked. We epitomized the meaning of "happy campers."

We lived in that rinky-dink park model for close to a year, if you can believe that. Our three girls were all five and under, so we bedded them on mattresses stacked on top of storage tubs in the itty-bitty bedroom. Phillip and I slept on blow-up twin mattresses on the floor in the mini living room, which I keenly piled on top of one another to serve as a couch during the day. We had no landline, no internet, no cell phone service, no T.V., barely any neighbors, and were at least 20 miles from town. I kid you not, we had more peace and joy living that simplistic lifestyle than we ever imagined. You could say that we went from living perfect to pleasant, as the campground was ironically located in Pleasant Valley.

Once Phillip got his strength back, it was time to leave our pleasantly peaceful haven in the valley of South Georgia and get busy pursuing our dream of empowering others to be healed, delivered, and set free. We wanted to establish a place where people could come and experience the same miraculous transformation that God had done in us. So, in 2004, we loaded up our sweet little girls in a moving truck to homestead on my family's 200 acres in East Texas, which for some strange reason my family called The Farm, even though it wasn't a farm at all. We had high hopes of building a retreat center there. We sadly sold Bubba truck and the tiny trailer, which held so many pleasant memories and left them behind in Georgia.

Miraculously beating death and depression through the finished work of Christ there at that remote church in South Georgia and living that quaint, simplistic life in Pleasant Valley had changed us in the most extraordinary way.

It settled some deep truths inside our souls about ourselves, each other, our Savior, the Adversary, the actuality of an unseen realm puppeteering the real, the reason we were alive, and what truly matters in life. A part of me wished we could have frozen that year in time, so we could feel that carefree and happy forever.

As I look back now, I most assuredly realize that was not the point at all. The meaning behind our experience was to permanently establish the spoils of our victories from the battles we'd fought and won over our lives and marriage—our solidarity as a couple, a family, our purpose as a unit, and our identity cemented in Christ as sons and daughters. A new greatheartedness settled over us that we'd only read about in the Bible or history books of the heroic men and women whose lives yielded a resiliency, sufficiency, relentless faith, radical generosity, uncommon peace and joy, along with daily courage because they'd overcome great hardship. That's who we now identified with. We were leaving that place as unsung heroes, who would go on to live undauntingly vulnerable and authentic lives.

These are the keys to remaining grounded in the twists and turns, mountaintops and valleys of this life in order to forever have the ability to distinguish what once was from what will never be again, in light of Christ's redeeming power.

In that moment, it was a hard goodbye. Our journey back west was quite somber. We mainly rode in silence, marveling at all we had overcome in the past couple of years. We were headed back older and wiser. We felt the triumph of no longer being that young married couple with fragile hopes of remaining together and making an impression on the world that we once were. A part of us had been awakened that we either had never known or that had been forgotten—a part of us that exuded brave assurance and fierce confidence to stand alone and stare down our enemies. I can only imagine that's what soldiers might feel like going home, after a long fight to win a war. This foreign gal inside of me felt gritty, gutsy, raw, and real like she'd really been through something and was done with the fake, the fluff, and performing for acceptance and approval. I felt ready for whatever life wanted to throw at me and ruined for ordinary. Bring it on!

Along with this brave new me, came a passion that was brewing inside me that I had never experienced before. It made me feel like grabbing a bullhorn and running through the streets yelling, "Wake up!" but I knew it wasn't time. Whatever was brewing needed a few more years to ferment. Right now, my job was yelling, "Wake up sleepy-heads, dinner's ready or it's bedtime!" and focusing on doing the mommy years well. How could I have forgotten about being a mommy, when I had a little boy inside me, kicking and punching to get out, and a belly ready to pop. I forgot to tell you that our little boy was just ten weeks away from his due date.

Our ideal plan of arrival to my family's land in Texas was to quickly settle in my parent's furnished, unlived-in mobile home, and store our belongings in the barn. Now, this wasn't just any mobile home, folks. It was what you call a double-wide. This plan of convenience was going to be so helpful, since the date for delivering our fourth and final child, the long-awaited son, was just around the corner.

However, when we pulled up to that trailer that hadn't been lived in for over two years, our happy hearts sank at the sight of it sitting in overgrown weeds with a giant, bright blue tarp on top covering all the holes in the roof. It looked like a nightmare on wheels and when we opened the front door to peek in, critters scurried!

Phillip is a git-r-done kind of guy. He discovered my Papaw's old tool shed, opened an account at the local hardware store, and had that wheeled nightmare whipped into a livable, baby-ready home with two weeks to spare from the delivery date. It wasn't an easy task or a pleasant experience. If he was telling the story, he would not spare the gory details.

Anyway, our baby boy arrived in October of 2004, and lit up our lives. He was the first baby we ever had that arrived on their due date. However, he had some health complications that kept him in the hospital his first month of life, which really helped us test-drive our newfound relentless faith. It's a story I hope to share one day, but for now, I'll just say, we came out of that experience more focused than ever on sharing our story of God's healing power. Bringing home that baby boy was another check-off on our dream list, adding fuel to the forward momentum of our new mission.

Our next matter of business was to form a non-profit called Get Real Ministries and start getting our story out "there" somehow. I'm not sure how it transpired; it's a phenomenon to me, but Phillip began to get invitations and booked for speaking engagements. I couldn't figure out how people even found us or knew where we were way out there in the country. We didn't have social media back then and the World Wide Web wasn't that sophisticated yet. However, just like that, he was hitting the road or jet-setting around the U.S. almost every weekend to speak and teach for whoever would have him.

A few years in, he was traveling overseas to minister as well. It was kind of crazy how ministry just took off for us. It was a little hard having him away so much, probably more for the kids than me, since I'm more the independent type, but an extra set of hands and eyes sure was always helpful and welcomed, and help was on its way.

A few months later, my parents moved back from Tulsa, bought a small trailer house to park right beside ours and I had all the help I could get—another check-off on my dream list. To make it even dreamier, Phillip and my dad built a wooden walkway, which the kids thought looked like a long, adventurous bridge, from the front door of our trailer to the back door of my parent's trailer. The kiddos could skip and hop across the bridge to my parents' home any time they wanted. It was an ideal set-up. The littles could roll out of bed in the morning and run to Papaw's, who loved cooking breakfast, especially fun-shaped pancakes with a story to go with them. My parents loved nothing more than to be with their grandbabies, so they were excited anytime we asked if they would keep them. This made it possible for me to travel with Phillip on occasion, which we loved, me especially. It was definitely a win-win situation for us all, and a special season of mine and my children's lives that will not soon be forgotten.

Even though I got to travel with Phillip every once-in-while, I must admit that I struggled with being envious of the exciting life he seemed to be leading; being flown all around the country, standing on stages telling our story, and getting wined and dined extravagantly. Meanwhile, I was at home leading the stay-at-home, fun, yet mundane, mommy life of naps, diapers, laundry, cooking, cleaning, doctor visits, more diapers and laundry, ballet, gymnastics, and bedtime stories. The same things day-in-and-day-out went the merry-go-round of my life at home in the double-wide.

As if I didn't already have enough mommy jobs, I also took it upon myself to maintain our personal and ministry finances, insurance, taxes, and any other administrative job I could think of to eliminate any stress from Phillip on the road. So, all he had to do when he was home was recoup, work on his book, and enjoy the kids. Wow, did I ever do a number on myself with that act of servitude. It didn't take too much time busting my fanny doing all that, when I began to feel tinges of resentment rising. Then, he'd get back from a trip, we'd have our private little welcome-home party, and I'd be all better for a while. See, there was this one little thing that I loved about him traveling so much. *Shh!* Now don't tell anybody I said this, but the welcome-back-home, I-missed-you-like-crazy sex was a-mazing! *Y'all know what I'm sayin'?*

While you're still recovering from the sex comment, I'm going to switch the subject to God and get reverent, in hopes to reign your thoughts back in. So, here we go, folks, back to the story now.

Living on my family's land, way out in the country, thirty minutes from civilization and the nearest town with stores, lent itself to lots of time with God. We didn't have a church fellowship or any friends to speak of either, which I was completely content with, versus what my life was like in Tulsa, where I obsessed over how many friends I had or who liked me. Not having friends to impress or a church to perform for during this season in Texas, freed up time and desire for intimacy with God like I'd never known. It began with me praying for Phillip while he was on the road and turned into me interceding for all his ministry engagements. I quickly developed a craving to spend time with God in intercession, waking up in the wee hours of the morning to be with Him before the world was awake.

While my family lay sleeping, I went on great adventures in the spirit with the Holy Spirit. It took praying from a prayer list to an entirely different level. It felt more like I was pulling down Heaven to earth; literally, assisting God in the spirit with solving huge matters in the natural world. It was honestly a time in my life that was so satisfyingly incredible that it is hard to put into words. Mainly because many would find it unbelievable and that would feel so dishonoring to this privileged season that I was honored to share with the God of the Universe.

My point in sharing this part of my story is to emphasize how laying down performance in my real-time life and ending the hustle for worthiness in my human relationships created space for me to have this dreamy relationship with the Savior. I flipped all my old, useless, time-consuming efforts of searching for love into an affinity with the Heavenly Father that I could have never conjured up in my wildest fantasies to fulfill my deepest of deep desires the way this season with God did.

It marked me forever with the truth of a life lived in the spirit and the legitimate power of prayer.

It also caused a desire to love Phillip from an unselfish place, which made our time together seem almost divine, like what God really intended for marriage. It also caused me to see that I could be just as useful to the Lord at home, away from the crowds, as I perceived Phillip was ministering to the masses. We were living the dream on a little piece of heaven!

Although I thought his life was glamorous and extravagant, Phillip missed being at home. I used to joke that we should just trade lives. I would gladly travel the world, standing on stages, eating fancy food, while he stayed home changing diapers, cooking, cleaning, and running kids to school. His solution, however, was to buy a travel trailer and big 'ole SUV to tow it, so the little ones and I could travel with him. We did and it was one of the best decisions we ever made. We had such a good time hauling our home-away-from-home around the country and making memories. It felt so right for all of us to be together and ministering together, like we were serving the purpose of our union and the family we'd built together.

One summer, we traveled 8,000 miles. There was just something about loading our family and all of our road trip stuff up in that big ole' SUV with a trailer in tow and shutting out the world that felt so comforting and brought so much peace. It was probably the relief that came from knowing we could stop hustling for worthiness for a minute, take a vacation from performing, and just breathe and be us.

Our ministry grew pretty quick after publishing our first book, *Get Real with God.* We formed a small staff and nice size following, too. So, what did we do? We started a church. It's quite humorous to look back on the buildings and businesses we "borrowed" with enough space to hold a service, once our little congregation outgrew our office space. We could have called it a Pop-Up Church, if we were running it today. We met in our house, in a café, in a bank, and we even met in a gym. The funniest place we popped up in with our church-in-a-box was a hair salon. LOL!

Those were fun times, full of fun memories doing what we loved. Phillip was living the life of ministry that he'd dreamed of, seeing folks healed and set free. Once, all the young'uns were in school, I started waiting tables at the café where we had church, and teaching group fitness classes at the gym, another place we had held church. The kiddos loved living next door to their Grammy and Papaw and putting on after-dinner shows for us every night. It all seemed a little too good to be true, honestly. Every now and then, I caught myself wondering when the perfect little snow-globe-of-a-life we were leading was going to crack. Even though we weren't fighting anymore, and I had become everything I thought Phillip fantasized about—super fit, sexual, and spiritual—he still seemed distant. Sometimes at night, when he was gone somewhere on a trip, the kids were asleep and I was up late doing laundry; I would pull out one of his shirts, hold it up to my face, and breath in his smell in an attempt to feel close to him, and wonder, "Would I ever be enough?"

Not everything was going as we'd hoped for with our ministry plans either. Five years of traveling left Phillip feeling like he was missing out on the children growing up. We and our staff were also growing weary trying to get our dream of a transformation center/ retreat off the ground. No matter what attempts we made with the city or country to get approval to build, we just hit walls and it started to feel like maybe it wasn't meant to be. Then oddly, things with our ministry began to shift, like staff started to move back home. So, we ended our Pop-Up church, and we shut down any building plans. We even started to feel like we should move to get the kids in a better school district. We felt the winds of change blowing, but weren't sure what direction they were leading.

After a lot of praying and seeking the Lord for what He wanted us to do next, we got offered a job with a church back in Georgia to come build and run their transformation center. The offer sounded like God to us. Phillip leaped at the thought of coming off the road. This job was to help establish a church plant in Atlanta, for one of the most ground-breaking church ministries in the world at the time (in my mind, anyway). For us, it was like wannabe actors being invited to Hollywood, so I'll reference this church as the Hollywood Church from here. When we prayed about the decision, we felt like we heard the Lord say where He was taking us was our "Dreamland." That was fitting, since this was a dream job offer. Who wouldn't want to live in Dreamland? Once we accepted the offer, we agreed that Phillip should move ahead of the kids and me to secure us a home.

Want to take a stab at what he found for a bargain basement deal? You guessed it, another trailer. It was this huge four-bedroom, three-bath, double-wide on the outskirts of Peachtree City, Georgia, which is this exclusive golf cart community ranked, at the time, in the top ten safest cities in America. The city's nickname was "The Bubble" and you could buy these cute little stickers that said, "Life in the Bubble" with a golf cart on it. I couldn't even believe such a place would even have a mobile home park, honestly. Lucky for us, it did; all tucked away behind a big shopping center, hidden by sweet, Georgia pines on the outskirts of town. It was a miracle that Phillip even found it, and an even bigger deal that we bought it in repossession for only $20,000. That's more than some people's cars, right?

A board member bought it for us, and Phillip fixed it up while he was waiting for the kids to get out of school so we could all be together again. In our discussions about buying the trailer, we never once wondered how it might affect our image, as it was no big thing to live in a mobile home in Texas. There, it's common for folks in the wide-open spaces of the big state to buy a piece of property and drop a trailer on it to live in while they were building a home. We thought it was actually a wise, non-committal choice, while we dreamed of and shopped for a permanent home to invest in. Not only was it cheap as heck, but the name of the mobile home park was Shiloh, which means *peace,* in the biblical sense. That sounded like just what we were searching for.

When school let out, me, my parents and the kids loaded up what was left of our belongings in a small, pull-behind storage trailer. My dad needed something to hold all of our stuff in place so he could secure the door to the storage trailer. He asked me to quickly find a piece of wood. So, I ran to our back porch, grabbed what appeared to be some random, blank piece of would, hurried it back to my dad, and he set it down to serve as a barrier between our stuff and the door. As soon as my dad stepped back to reach for the doors, I could read what was painted on the other side of the wood, "DREAMLAND."

I was astonished. It was a sign the girls had painted to hang over their playhouse a few years prior, which I had completely forgotten about.

With that, I told them to get in the car and get buckled up. Apparently, we were headed to Dreamland, just like the Lord said. I kid you not, for half the way there, we passed billboards advertising *Dreamland Barbeque*, in big, eye-catching letters. I'm so not kidding. It was a little unbelievable. When we rolled into the Shiloh Mobile Home Park in Peachtree City, GA, where our new home on wheels was parked, I can't say that I thought it looked like Dreamland by any stretch of the imagination, but I remained hopeful. Phillip's excitement to see us, the welcome posters he had made, and the dinner he had cooked us was dreamy enough for the time being.

Things were unusually peaceful living there for the first year or so, kind of like the calm before the storm. Our family was loving our new community and enjoying getting acclimated to the area. We especially loved the golf cart trails that would lead you anywhere in the city. We bought a bright yellow one to match our new happy life and jumped right into living the golf cart life "in the bubble." We were all meeting lots of new people from church and school. In fact, we made more friends our first year in Peachtree City, than we had our entire lives. I loved it! We were also having people over for dinner often or throwing big birthday parties for our kid's birthdays and inviting lots of people to our mobile home in the trailer park without image issues to speak of. We didn't care about where we lived or what we lived in. We were just happy to be alive and together, grateful to be living in such a cool community, super excited about our new job, having fun driving our golf cart, and anticipating what God had in store for us in Dreamland.

Living in a mobile home, came to an end after a decade. For nostalgia's sake, I refer to them as the trailer years. But vacationing in a camper/trailer will probably last a lifetime. We prefer to call it our vacation home on wheels because it's taken us wherever we've wanted to get-away—the beach, the mountains, to the lake, or the river. I still say it's the best purchase we've ever made and also contains some of the best memories we've ever made. Like I mentioned before, there's just something about piling all my kids and dogs up in those tight quarters and closing the camper door behind us that feels like you're shutting out the world.

It's a little more challenging these days to get everyone piled in there, because my kiddos are grown, with lives of their own, and spouses or sweethearts. But my motive for wanting to shut out the world is different now. I don't want or need a breather from perfecting and performing. Now, it's because I'm in love with the intimacy and connection I have with my family when we are all cram-packed and cozied up together to share, laugh, munch, lounge, and just be. I love the quote from a wooden sign that I saw in a camping store a couple of years ago: "A crowded camper is better than an empty castle."

It sounds just awful now, but I used to daydream about the time when all my kids were gone, and I could keep my house perfect all the time. These days I prefer it a little loud, kind of messy, and a bit crowded—that's where the love is.

Summary

Now, I feel like I need to close out this chapter with a disclosure statement. Those years of uncommon peace and crazy faith that I just described were not the product of perfection by any means. Nor were they because we had no challenges or were without problems, we had plenty. Instead, we chose to stand in truth and not allow them to bowl us over or cause our faith to buckle under the weight of them, like they used to when we had no skills to navigate them. We were different now with our eyes wide open, with new perspectives and values from surviving and winning a war. We'd learned to live greathearted—loved, faithful, resilient, confident, and courageous—bendable, but no longer breakable. We had learned to make pain and struggle our friend. It was messy and uncomfortable, yet we'd allowed the tension of them to push us to take huge risks. The rewards of those risks were peace and faith, but even better than that, was a new lease on life gifted to us by God when we didn't even deserve it. That, my friends, is called, grace. No, we were anything but perfect and our troubles were far from over.

What have you learned from reading our story and walking with us through our trials, challenges, and struggles?

How have struggles caused you to grow closer to your spouse?

How did you handle the key transitions of having kids, job changes, moving, loss, big disappointments, setbacks, kids leaving home, or retirement?

How has your "crazy" faith or lack of faith affected your marriage journey?

Chapter 9

LIVING IN DREAMLAND
IN THE SPOTLIGHT

Darlena

What Perfection Was Doing to Us

For me, even though moving to Georgia, aka, Dreamland was what I had felt God directed us to do, starting over and trying to win friends and influence people in such a performance-driven community, honestly, revved the engine of perfection in me and drove me into a lifestyle of hiding, again. However, I didn't realize it until I crashed and burned. It only took about a year and a half for my life in the bubble to burst. It felt similar to our first year of marriage, it was a slow fade.

The honeymoon phase ended when after three months of living in the bubble, the Hollywood church hit us with a low blow to the gut, telling us they could no longer hire us. It's kind of a sorted story, but the gist of it was that they received news from the "mother church" in California that they were not allowed to hire us because we hadn't been through their school of ministry. So, there could be no guarantee that we would be on board with their mission and therefore, not a suitable prospect for hire. We chose to stop going to church there. So, we found ourselves a long way away from home without a job and no church family to bring a sense of security and stability. However, we weren't without any leads, thank goodness.

A good many folks knew us from our ministry because Phillip had taught at a couple of churches in the area. It really helped that a few key people already knew us because those folks introduced us to their circle of friends. The next thing we knew, we're being invited to try out our new life course, *The Jordan Crossing*, at local churches and home fellowships around the area. There was a synergy around what we were teaching and the excitement about what we were bringing to the community helped us course-shift. This led us to launch a local counseling ministry in an office space that someone graciously blessed us with. Without being aware of it, we'd developed a small, local following and started partnering with churches in the area and became a sort of para-church ministry. This eventually led to marriage counseling. The more Phillip researched this topic to hone his skills, the more he realized that we had some serious work still to be done on our own marriage.

Who has time to work on your marriage when your family homestead is on fire? Yes, you read right. Just nine months after moving from our home in Texas, it caught fire. It was such a blazing fire with long, reaching flames, that it caught everything around it on fire. This included my parents' house, a three-car garage, the old tool shed out back, our former offices which were built above the shed, and the saddest thing of all, our personal storage building.

I'm tearing up just trying to write about it. All our memories and sentimental things from our childhood to our children's early years (before everything went digital) were turned to ashes. My wedding dress, wedding pictures, college photo albums, mission trip scrapbooks, videos of the kids, and all the baby pictures of my sweet girlies were gone. Anything that had been specially collected, like holiday décor, fancy dinnerware, silver stemware, antique depression glass, all melted into the East Texas black dirt. We had left anything that we thought wasn't necessary for starting a new life Georgia behind in Texas. I'll never forget wrestling with the decision to take this one and only red storage tub, which contained every single photograph I had ever taken of my baby girls. Every picture that I had beat myself up over for not putting in a scrapbooking album was in it. Side Note: I was so obsessed with being perfect, that I could never get myself to do scrapbooking or even write in the kid's baby books. So, they remained packed in the red tub. I literally put it in and took it out of that dang U-Haul I don't know how many times trying to decide if I should take it or leave it. Obviously, I left it. If I ever got a chance to go back in time, I would get that red tub and carry it into eternity with me! I have never been so mad at myself in all my born days and couldn't even begin to tell you how many times I've replayed that scene in my mind. To this day, I can't see a red tub and not think about it.

Because our office burned as well, Phillip lost his entire ministry library, all his original teaching CD's, and all our ministry related info saved on three computer hard drives. Not to mention all that my family lost because they were actually living there. I can't even write about it. Needless to say, it was an insurmountable loss for us all.

My sweet, daddy, bless his heart, watched the entire place burn to the ground without a thing he could do about it. The local volunteer fire department took an hour to arrive, so by the time they showed up, all the buildings were ablaze, and the fire was out of control. All that was left of the homestead were the wheels and axles of the two trailer houses and my melted depression glasses.

Daddy was mentally, emotionally, and physically traumatized from the experience. He had a massive heart attack a few weeks later and had major by-pass surgery that took six weeks for him to recover from. He regained himself physically, but not mentally, and eventually developed dementia. He's in a nursing home today. Hard stuff can make one's heart hard, if not handled carefully and intentionally. I for one, did not handle it well. Initially, I surprisingly did not even shed a tear at the news of the fire or my daddy's heart attack. However, there was an emotional build-up taking place on the inside of me that was going to get ugly when it came out. It started like a slow-dripping faucet that eventually turned into a gusher with every little thing that went wrong hereafter.

The Slow-Dripping Faucet

Back on the home front, the girls were in their second year of school, in the bubble—two in middle school and one in elementary—and had begun riding the bus home to and from school. One afternoon, early in the school year, my middle school daughters get off the bus with the younger one, Lydia, crying. She told me through her tears that some of the kids on the bus, from the nice neighborhoods, had made fun of her for living in a trailer park. My heart just broke for her. There is little else I detest more in this life that bullying or shaming innocent people. So, my stomach was curdling. Then she begged me to never make her ride the bus again. Wish granted. Never again. *Can you hear my emotional faucet dripping?*

In the meantime, I had joined the PTO and felt myself getting more and more vague about where we lived, after I unmistakably recognized some of the women's appalled looks, once I disclosed that we lived in the mobile home park. *Drip. Drip.*

Then, my youngest daughter, who was still in elementary school, insisted she keep riding the bus. She gets off another afternoon in late fall with a little attitude and a story to tell. With her little hand on her hip, she tells me how she was called "trailer trash" by some kids at school. All my momma bear buttons got pushed over that. I can call myself and my kids trailer trash when I'm joking, but nobody gets to call my kid that for real. *Do you know what I'm talking about?* I was so riled up over my little girl being degraded like that in front of other kids, I felt I could've seriously hurt somebody if I wasn't a dignified lady poser. That disclosure crap from Chapter 8 about being resilient, faithful, and unbreakable, well, it got trashed right about here. There was none of that greathearted nonsense going on in my heart or head in this moment.

I was getting close to the gushing point. The drip had turned into a steady flow. I was feeling very edgy all the time. Phillip, well, he was practicing distance.

By year three in the trailer park, our daughters had hit puberty, so of course, they had become more image-conscious. We noticed them starting to want to go to their friend's houses, instead of inviting them to ours. After lots of questioning, they reluctantly admitted to being embarrassed to bring their friends to the trailer park when all of them lived in such nice neighborhoods. I did not blame them. I shared that I had stopped inviting friends over for the same reason and was growing green with envy every time I was invited to a friend's big, beautiful house with a luscious lawn and well-groomed neighborhood with a water park for a clubhouse. Our confessions were terribly hard for Phillip to hear and caused him to feel ashamed for allowing our family to live there surrounded by poverty and darkness. On the other hand, I just got pissed and started thinking about how God said He was moving us to Dreamland. What did He mean by that? Because life in this run-down, low-life trailer park was no Dreamland. It was beginning to feel and look more like a Wasteland. What the heck?

Then, just like that, it was as if the sands of time stood still for a brief moment, and in my mind's eye I got a picture of man like The Great and Powerful Oz from *The Wizard of Oz*, emerge from behind a heavy, dark curtain and declare in a deep, rumbling tone, "The years of peace have come to an end!" I suddenly felt the urge to get drunk. I raised a big stink with Phillip, went storming out of the house, bought a four-pack of mini wine bottles and a box of Krispy Kreme doughnuts, too. *Yeah, this is probably a good spot to confess that I'm a wuss when it comes to drinking, so it didn't take much to get me sloshed.* I parked in a remote area of a parking lot, sat in my car, eating and drinking myself sick. Then, I went home, fumbled my way into the house and to our bedroom, where I flopped on the floor beside our bed and began to wail. Phillip, honorably, came to check on me.

I told him that life wasn't fair and that I just wanted to die. I also whimpered that it was all his fault that we were in this horrible situation we were in. I blubbered that if he had never accepted that job offer from the Hollywood church, then we would have never left Texas. Then I blamed the Hollywood church for teasing us with a job to get our whole family to move to the ghettos of that ridiculously uppity, fake, out-of-our-league, bubble of a community, just to kick us to the curb once we got there. *See, I told you it was going to be a gusher.* I flooded our entire trailer house with dammed up grief, disappointment, regret, and bitter envy. It was ugly, just like I said.

Feeling the aftershock of that riveting night, the sting of relationship conflicts with new friends we'd been trying to please, and the
unrelenting pressure of living in such a performance-driven community, we started feeling ourselves plummeting back into a lifestyle of
hiding and hustling for worthiness. The feuding between Phillip and
I commenced once again. The bingeing and numbing out, once our
familiar friends, moved back in. The blame games resumed; I blamed
him for not making enough money to give us the lifestyle I wanted,
and of course for moving us there in the first place. He blamed me
for spending too much that kept us in debt. The resentment settled
back in like an old companion.

We both started feeling discontent with the direction our lives had
taken and with our marriage. We were ashamed of living in a low-life
trailer in a wretched mobile home park in one of the most exclusive
cities in middle Georgia, fondly known as The Bubble. We reclaimed
stakes in the pervasive lie of the American dream that money, status,
looks, and things lead to happiness. I had become so sick of going
to my friend's beautiful big homes in plush neighborhoods, that I
felt like heaving as soon as I approached their house. The "keeping
up with the Jones" thing was literally starting to make me feel crazy.
I could feel depression breathing down my neck. The country club
fantasy started taunting me, for old times sake.

What I had somehow missed, overlooked, or just didn't matter
when we first moved into the mobile home park, I now had eyes to
see—run-down cars, rusty old trailers, front yards that look like the
houses threw up, foreigners everywhere, countless Mexicans packed
in one house, jacked-up cars with lightening down the sides, kids
running around unattended, teenagers that looked like zombies, and
dirty old men that stared at me and my daughters.

For the first time, I was keenly aware of the difference between me and the other moms that stood at the bus stop. Most of them were either overweight or sickly skinny and looked hungover and either unashamedly dressed in pajamas with bedhead or drenched in black, tattooed up with a greasy ponytail, occasionally sporting a beer. Without fail though, they all wore house shoes and had cigarettes dangling from their lips. Whilst perching myself a safe distance from the squalor, I would always be decked out from head to toe in the latest fashion and embellished with accessories from Target (that would be pronounced Tar-zhay) and a Starbucks coffee.

Then, while waiting at the bus stop and checking out the house shoe club in disgust as they stood on the corner all slouched over their cigarettes, I suddenly heard the Sesame Street song from childhood playing in my head that went something like this, "This one here is not like the other, this one here just doesn't belong…" And not two seconds later, I overheard two of the mom's talking loud enough for me to hear.

The overweight one in her white bathrobe and pink bunny house shoes with bedhead said to the mom dressed in all black, dyed black hair, heavy black eye-liner, and leopard print house shoes with a cigarette hanging out of her mouth, "Darlena is always dressed so cute, every day."

"Yeah, I know. Darlena lives **in** the trailer park, but she's not **of** the trailer park."

I, of course, responded with a polite thank you, albeit the half-hearted, looking-down-my-nose kind. Then "ding," a lightbulb went off in my head and I thought to myself, "She's right! I don't belong here! So, why in the heck am I living here then? Somebody get me out of here!"

I was freaked out by that bus stop incident. From that moment on, I was praying my guts out for our finances to increase, so we could stop living in a dang trailer and get the heck out of squalor holler. So, my kids would never be called trailer trash again, I would never have to wait at the bus stop with those atrocious women, and we wouldn't be ashamed of where we lived. *I know this sounds harsh and judgmental, but it was where I was at. Just being real.*

I had become a bear to live with. To numb out, I was eating drive-thru food nearly every day, which adversely affected my health. The emotional stress combined with the awful eating had me feeling drained and lethargic with heavy brain fog. Most days, I was falling asleep at my desk. I was bickering with the girls so much that you couldn't tell from listening in, who the adult was. Phillip was working a night job, teaching at a local college. When he was home, he was quiet and disengaging. There was zero happening in our bedroom, but I was still praying.

Then, *hallelujah, to thine be the glory*, our ship came in! I'll fill in the details in a minute. The quick version is our popularity went up, our finances tripled, and we had enough money for a down payment on a house, which at the time, had become an obsession. Not just any ole' lived-in home, either. We really went for it and chose to *build* a new home (while the market was down and we got a steal of a deal, of course). Whoever that Oz guy was in my head that day, didn't know what the heck he was talking about. Everything could only get better because we were moving up in the world. Not to embellish things too much, but life went so well for us that particular year, I am certain that the friends and family who received our annual family Christmas pic/update letter undoubtedly wanted to barf. Enough said.

I thought that moving out of the trailer house would be one of the happiest days of my life. Instead, it was quite sobering. I went by myself to do a last clean sweep after Phillip and some guy friends moved all the furniture out. While sweeping, I found seven dimes in different spots—no pennies or any other coins. I kept them all to show Phillip later because I thought it was a little weird and wondered if maybe it meant something, as I'm a little weirdly into numbers and their spiritual significance. I wondered if the Lord was trying to send me a message or make a point with them.

As I was wrapping things up, I began to feel convicted for the nasty attitude I'd developed over the past couple of years, blaming Phillip for my unhappiness and all the judgmental things I'd thought or said about the house shoe moms at the bus stop, the snooty moms at PTO, the leaders at the Hollywood church, and how I'd even judged God for tricking me with the promise of Dreamland. When I went to leave the trailer for the last time, I paused to have one last look around to reminisce about the humbling good times we'd had there and to revel in the gratitude of breaking ground on our brand new house, very aware that I was once again, closing another chapter of my life. Although I wanted to feel ecstatic, I heard that Mr. Oz voice again in my head, like a warning to get ready for what was ahead.

My reaction surprised me, rather than fear and dread, I felt the rumble of greatheartedness from deep within me. I was assured that whatever lay ahead of me, with God's strength I would victoriously overcome.

Our house was scheduled to be done in three months, which just happen to be during summer break, perfect timing. We had planned to live in our camper at a nearby campground, but our friends wouldn't have it. Two, of which, were empty nesters with very large beautiful homes and could accommodate our large family, insisted we live with them during the interim. We worked out a plan together—we would live for six weeks in one home and six weeks in the other. Perfect! Both homes looked like they'd come straight out of a magazine with a pool, game rooms, and the works. One of them had seriously been a set for the movie, *What to Expect When You're Expecting*. The kiddos thought this was a hoot and had all our friends and family back home watching the movie. It felt more like we were vacationing in luxury resorts for the summer. This was going to be such a fun summer… maybe, for the kids.

One last thing before we literally close this chapter of my life, the dime finding thing continued. I would find them every day and in the wildest ways and places. I found them all around the houses we lived in that summer, in parking lots, in stores, public restrooms, and randomly on the ground anywhere I happened to be walking indoors or outside. The weirdest times were when I would wake up and there would be a dime laying in a spot that there was no dime the night before. I know, freaky, right? It got to where it happened so frequently that all I had to do was text Phillip, "Found another one," for him to know exactly what I was referring to. The most predominant feeling each time I have found one was hope, like it was bringing me a message of encouragement to not give up believing in my dream. Or in Dreamland, maybe? *Interesting, huh?*

After some anonymous person left a round silver tin full of dimes with my name on top, in the chair I typically sat in at church, I finally decided to look up the spiritual meaning of the number 10. Here's what I found: the number 10 represents fulfillment, attainment, and completion/completeness or full circle; what comes around goes around; perfection of Divine Order—the beginning of a new order. *Perfection, huh?* Well, we'll see how attaining "complete perfection" goes.

Phillip

Big transitions in life are not easy. Moving my family of six people to a new community where we didn't have a job or a permanent place to live sounded crazy at the time. We left-behind two-hundred acres, a free place to live, and my very supportive in-laws next door. That's hard to beat. Why leave? We felt like God was calling us to Georgia. I know that sounds brainless, but we lived our lives seeking after God's direction and choosing to follow His lead.

I dreamed about God answering my prayer to bring healing to our marriage and family. I saw this beautiful picture of myself with my wife and kids. We were in a beautiful southern home and the sunlight was brightly shining through the front windows. Darlena and the girls were dressed in white dresses and dancing in a circle to soft music. Wilson and I were laughing and clapping as they danced. Peace, abiding, real deep peace washed over me. This is what it looked like to have Heaven in my home. That vision stayed with me during this season and it became my prayer. I would have heaven in my home and a home where heaven dwells. I thought when we moved to Georgia everything would fall into place and life would be sweet, like milk and honey.

Like the children of Israel, we were being called to a promise land or dreamland as Darlena put it. However, we had very different versions of what that meant for us. I wanted the security of being on staff at a church and fulfilling my purpose in ministry. Darlena wanted to have a nice home, a great school system for the kids, and a community of friends to surround us. We envisioned God waving a wand and meeting all our needs in abundance. When we didn't get the job and we couldn't buy the house, we found ourselves complaining that God wasn't doing His part.

I felt controlled by Darlena's dissatisfaction. It was all my fault that we weren't living in Dreamland. I felt responsible for moving our family across the country, again. I hated the conversations that quickly turned into conflict about our situation. It sounded to me like she was moaning and complaining and unwilling to help me make it better. My ears were fixed on her grumbling. So, I chose to avoid her and the subject.

My tendency was to try harder when things didn't work out for us. I did everything I could to make life better for us. I took on everything that I could to generate money for the family including working on a horse farm on the weekends. At the same time, I poured my heart into every ministry opportunity. The number one goal in my mind was for us to do life together as a family unit. That meant I would no longer travel to do ministry. Choosing to stay home with my family and grow a local ministry was a drastic budget cut. I went from generating six figures to making barely enough to live on month to month. It was a major blow to my ego as a man, but I was committed to being present in my home. I know we were living on poverty row, but I stayed committed to doing life together as a family.

The big challenge for me was that I felt responsible for Darlena's emotional ups and downs. I told myself that if I was a better provider then she would have been more stable. Her burden became my ball and chain. I personalized her bellyaching. I took my usual path to solving the problem. I shut down, pulled away, and blamed her for being a stiff-necked un-submissive wife.

The grind of these middle years was monotonous and draining. The harder I tried to get something going, the worse things were. I desperately tried to get our ministry off the ground in this new community. The struggle was strangling my hope and I was beginning to think that moving to Georgia was a big mistake.

God's favor saved the day. Once again, something happened that only God deserved the credit for. He opened the door for us to become the senior leader at a local church. The timing was perfect. This opportunity gave me confidence that God was at work preparing us for something special.

Summary

The Promise Land/Dreamland was a big part of our fantasy. The illusion was we would move from Texas to Georgia and land the dream job which would give us the money to buy the finest house in the second-to-none neighborhood with award-winning schools that would help us create perfect children. I believed I couldn't have heaven in my home until I made these things happen. The fantasy of owning a big beautiful home and the great high-paying job was part of the trap of perfection. We hide behind our insulated walls and our self-important positions. A nice house and a good job are no substitute for love and belonging. We needed to realize that God was calling us to a promised land that was not filled with stuff to make us happy, but relationships that were secure because we learned how to love one another without performance demands or buying stuff to make us happy.

What would your Dream Land look like?

How would your Dream Land offer security and significance?

How do you react when Dream Land turned into Realityville?

Chapter 10
DONE

Darlena

We were certain Dreamland awaited us on the other side of us moving into that brand-spanking-new house, which we were building from the ground up with hand-written scriptures on the foundation. It felt like the waiting lasted an eternity, taking nearly six months until it was finished. The kids were having a blast living in the resort-like homes, but it made me a nervous wreck. I stayed anxious that my little guy would break something, the girls would spill something, the Yorkie would pee on the carpet, the kids would leave their fingerprints on the glass doors or their barefoot prints on the glossy wooden floors that you could see when the sun hit it just right, and that my house cleaning skills were not up-to-par. The absolute worst part was the complete and utter fear that I lived in, that our friends might catch me yelling at the kids or bickering with Phillip. Or worse, witness me in a rage. That would be my worst nightmare and had me shaking in my boots.

Before I go any further, let me back up a little and fill you in on how we got to this point—how our proverbial ship came in since I left you hanging. Keep in mind that what I am about to tell you all happened within a span of a year. In 2011, we were gaining some momentum with our new life course, *The Jordan Crossing*, as Phillip shared in his version of our story. We were invited to lead a group at the CEO of Chick-fil-a's house. Not long after this, a friend of ours was a guest on, *Sid Roth's It's Supernatural*, and told him about our book. We get a call from a staff person of the show who asked us to overnight them a copy, which is only something we printed off our computer at this point. Low and behold, they loved it. They wanted to publish it for us and have us on the show. We were dumbfounded, to say the least. We were flown out to the film set that summer to pre-record the show. I about went looney trying to decide what to wear on the show. During the three days of filming, we sat in a green room with other well-known spiritual leaders that we had admired or followed over the years. That was quite surreal. To hear, "Quiet on the set!", for real was even wilder. Phillip and I have never watched the show from start to finish. We can't exactly say why, but I'm sure it has something to do with the fear of not showing up perfect.

Our book was released in the Fall of 2011. The show aired for 4 weeks in January of 2012. While the show was airing, we received approximately 250 calls and/or emails a day from the listeners asking for prayer or sharing how they related to our story. That was overwhelming. I laugh every time I think of this—I had to create a spot in my house, which is the trailer house in Peachtree City, to have privacy and quiet to return calls and emails. The master bathroom in that place was ridiculously large. So, I turned it into my office. I'd get people on the phone and when they'd find out it was really me, in person, they were shocked and treated me like I was some bigtime celeb. Meanwhile, I was trying not to burst out laughing because they have no idea "the celeb" was calling them from their toilet/office.

However, I was not laughing when folks wanted to fly in to have us minister to them in person. That was too much for me. I felt so much pressure to perform so they would have their expectations met of a miraculous healing.

So, becoming a T.V. star didn't make my life the envy of everyone I knew like I had fantasized it would. It was more like the beginning of the end for me. I began a slow emotional and spiritual decline from there.

In the Spring of 2012, Phillip was offered a lead pastor position of a small local church, one that he used to speak at a couple of times a year when he was an itinerate speaker. Our first Sunday was April Fool's Day that year. I personally felt so much pressure at the church for me to be perfectly amazing and cause the presence of the Lord to fall every Sunday that I dreaded going. I tried to be a part of the worship team but couldn't handle people looking at me in expectation. I felt like our family was being judged. I am not accusing anyone of making me feel this way, this was the narrative playing in my head. Some folks did make accusations about our children which caused them to not want to go anymore. Phillip, the poor man, had to drag us all to the church house every Sunday with our melancholy faces, which had to be so discouraging and exhausting. So, I tried to spare him the grief and shame of refusing to go to church. My solution was for me and the kids to all run the nursery, children's church, and youth ministry, which were conveniently all in the basement. No one else would volunteer to help, which gave us no other options, but to use our family. In turn, it created the perfect means for me to escape participating in the church services and enduring all the people's looks and stares and gestures that I perceived as judgment.

I thought I had finally gotten something right, until one of the attendees accused Phillip of Nepotism. *I know, what does that even mean? I'd never heard of it either.* Apparently, it's an old Latin word, formed centuries ago that means to grant employment in the church to family members regardless of merit. We told him we'd be happy to turn the positions over to him or anyone in his family who wanted to volunteer in our place, or maybe even give us a break every now and then, of which he responded with a no. The case was closed, after assuring him that none of us got paid except Phillip. *Okay, anybody want to be a pastor now?*

I realize I probably sound cynical, but honestly, it's next to impossible to work in the church or any system for years and not see and experience things that leave you believing that no matter what you do, you just can't get it right. Someone is always waiting in line to point out what you don't have perfect. Even so, I am very much aware that without the job at this church, we would not have been able to afford to move out of the trailer and build a beautiful new, never-lived-in-by anyone-else home. For that, I will always be grateful and feel blessed.

Speaking of home, we also ventured into the world of homeschooling our children through a small homeschool coop. It was very small, like everyone-knew-everything-about-everyone small. Now, I want to be clear that we did not start schooling our children at home because we had a huge conviction to do so. We did it to honor our oldest daughter's request. She came home from summer church camp claiming God told her she was to homeschool, so she could live a "set apart" life, like a Nazarite. Our response was, "Alrighty, then. I guess we will be withdrawing you from school. Yay!" When she came home, the rest of the girls wanted to come home. Well, we kind of had to coerce our youngest daughter. My point is to convey the fact that we homeschooled our children during the same time that we were pastoring the church and that homeschooling taxed the heck out of our marriage. I spent every waking moment lost in it, with zero time or energy for Phillip or anything else, for that matter.

We didn't become one of those weird, unsocialized stereotyped homeschool families. I can say that I have never been so out of my league in all my life than those three years I schooled my girls through the direction of a homeschool coop, while our little buddy attended public school. I thought one of the reasons folks schooled at home was to escape the high-pressure, competitive environment of public school. Oh, baby, was I wrong. When I walked through the doors of the church where the coop met, the perfection level was so high, I froze up and broke out in a sweat. *Can you even freeze and perspire at the same time?* I don't know, but that's how I felt. What I am trying to say is that I was extremely uncomfortable and intimidated around all the homeschool moms, totally out of my element. In fact, the environment made me feel worthless.

So, I had to dig deep to find what value I brought to the table, and here's what I came up with. I may not have been the most academic mom on the block, but you could bet me and my kids were the best-dressed homeschoolers those people had ever seen. I was nominated for Best Dressed, Greenville High School, 1984. I didn't win, but I have held that nominee position like a trophy ever since. It was my claim to fame for years, and I took pride in me and my family showing up and looking like we had just stepped out of a catalog. Anyway, my point is, some days I felt like all I could do well in the homeschool world was look good and teach my kids how to dress cute, be best dressed, and produce really great looking art projects, which got top of the class every time. Did I mention that I minored in art in college?

Now mind you, we were stuck in the basement of our friend's home for almost two months longer than we had expected, because of delays with our house and our financing, which was extremely nerve-wracking. We felt out of control of both of our living spaces, which was amping up our anxiety levels big time. We were whisper fighting like crazy. *Ever done that?* The couple we were living with were some of the sweetest folks you'll ever meet, but when they had to tell us we needed to be moved out before Thanksgiving, regardless, it was so awkward. While living there, it became very apparent that something was not right with me. The wife of the couple we lived with, who's like a mother to me, was the first to confront me about my unusual behavior, although I'm not sure if she was the first to notice. She observed that I rarely left the house anymore and stayed in my pajamas most days.

"Oh, God!" I thought, "I'm turning into a trailer park mom!" I needed to get some help before I took up smoking and wearing my fuzzy house shoes in public. First, I needed to confess to Phillip that I'd been trying to hide my crazy. Of course, he already knew, he just didn't want to face having to endure working through more of my emotional crap. I had to confess that I felt so disconnected from God that I didn't have anything to offer spiritually. So, I asked him to please not expect anything from me at church, not to pray for anyone, and especially not speak. When I fessed up to taking over the nursery, children's church, and youth ministry so I could hide out in the basement, it wasn't a news flash to him. He just looked at me, not knowing what to say, and I just felt ashamed and worthless.

So, there you have it—the year's bounty from our proverbial ship having come in. We were finally able to make our newly built house a home on November 9, 2012, which gave us official bragging rights for including it along with all those other glorious accomplishments, mentioned above, in our 2012 Christmas letter/pic. Here's a recap for you—we published our third book, were guests on an international Christian T.V. talk show, became lead pastor of a local church, had the coveted beach vacation with friends, and built a new house. They were all deliciously and delightfully listed along with the amazing achievements of our four darling children and impressive B.S. about how we were rocking it at homeschool. We were looking awesome in our Christmas picture, too. It was taken on the beach at sunset during our Florida vacation with friends. *You know the typical white shirt beach pictures, where everyone is looking all slap-happy from playing and drinking in the sun all day, and sunburned as heck?* Our letter that year was so outrageous, I am quite certain that every family member and old friend that made it to the end wanted to throw up a little.

My life may have seemed great on paper, but I was not feeling it on the inside. What I didn't realize at the time, was that I felt like our lives were under a microscope, and the closer the light came to our family's issues, the more I hustled for perfection. Doing life in all those small settings made me feel like all eyes were on me. The heat of it kept me in an anxious sweat. I expended so much energy attempting to make our family look flawless for everyone in our sphere of influence that I was physically, mentally, emotionally, and spiritually drained. For someone who spent every day armoring up so that they would not be seen, protecting themselves from shame or rejection, living under a microscope was like dying a slow, exhausting death, especially if that person had a core belief from childhood that said, "If you get found out, you will die."

I thought moving into our beautiful new home, would really help me improve emotionally, and it did for a while. The housewarming parties and all the Christmas festivities were a fun distraction from my inner turmoil. After the holidays when the newness wore off, I slipped back into a funk. It wasn't depression, I knew what that felt like. It was primarily serious brain fog, forgetfulness, inability to focus, and constant pressure in my head. I tried to play it off by getting really engrossed in decorating the house for a few months, then redecorating the church for another few months. That was how I "checked out"—getting busy. I thought I had the family fooled, but I'm sure my edginess and angry outbursts when things didn't go my way were a dead giveaway that all was not rosy with me.

The girls and I stayed in constant conflict, bickering heavily all day when Phillip was at work. We argued so much that the girls took to holing up in their bedrooms instead of us all doing school together in the dining room, like I insisted on when moved into the new house. I continued to try and hide all the fighting with the girls from Phillip, like when they were little. But unlike when they were little, they now told on me, and he could guess what had been going on all day because the tension was so thick in the house when he walked in from the office that you could cut in with a knife.

Things got so bad between Phillip and I that it seemed impossible to have a civil conversation. Even the simplest interactions turned into opportunities to spew anger at him. He stopped inviting me to lunch, which he did frequently when we first moved to Peachtree City. We stopped going on date nights because they just turned into arguments. We couldn't even have sex without turning it into an argument. One of the reasons being, I'd put on weight and felt uncomfortable with him seeing me without my clothes on. I even went into the closet and shut the door to change. It was bad.

The only thing we could do together or talk about without causing a dust-up (as Phillip refers to it), was to talk about other people. So, it got to where we spent hours ripping others up one side and down the other. It felt scary good to get all our pent-up bitterness and resentment out about all sorts of things to do with other people. I also felt bitterroot judgment set up camp in our hearts and in our home, which tainted the atmosphere even more. However, if we talked about much else, besides politics and the weather, it stirred up a fight. We upheaved our beautiful new home into a battle zone. No wonder, our girls locked themselves in their rooms.

One of his peacekeeping tactics was to avoid me as much as possible. He eventually started numbing out in front of the T.V. again, which turned into an every-night, after-dinner routine, until he went to bed. His T.V. watching made me fume inside. I literally hated it. I'm not sure why. Maybe because that's what both of our dads did when we were growing up, or maybe it was because I felt Phillip chose the T.V. over me. One of the reasons I kept myself busy at night when he was home was to block out the hostility I felt as a result of him watching T.V. Thoughts would rage through my mind about how he could be working on finishing his Ph.D. to make more money; or make wood projects in the garage with the stupid workshop that he painstakingly set up; or write one of the countless counseling curriculum that he ideated about incessantly; or maybe teach our son, Wilson, how to play football like he'd told him over and over that he would do.

For the love of God! Just do something with your life! Stop wasting your brain and your calling on that television! Those were also some of the nastier thoughts that raged through my mind and sometimes out of my mouth, if I got triggered. My heart rate went up, stomach knotted up, eyes widened, and lips twisted into a snarl, and out of my mouth came words that stabbed him in the heart like daggers. *I still get a little fired up just thinking about all those wasted years of watching T.V.*

It's not fun thinking back on the hard times or remembering old feelings. Writing this book has conjured up old feelings that I've had to keep surrendering to Jesus. I particularly have an acute aversion to thinking back on all the times in my past when I behaved so ghastly and beastly. It makes me feel queasy when I picture those instances and remember the frightened reactions of Phillip and my children, and what they must have been feeling. I have to diligently guard my heart against regret by choosing to live in redemption every day.

Wilson was my happy place. When the girls were in school, it was just me and him at home having fun. Now things had reversed—the girls were at home and he was at school. So, my favorite time of the day became when he came home in the afternoon. He was a joyful distraction from the tension that homeschooling the girls brought into each day. He was affectionate, kind, and thoughtful, always giving me compliments, telling me he loved me, and giving me hugs and kisses. Our relationship never became inappropriate. However, I'm sure I depended on him in an unhealthy way for the love and affection that I was not getting from Phillip, who had deemed me as unsafe and completely shut me out, again. There was no hugging, no kissing, no touching of any kind between him and me at this juncture of our marriage.

Phillip kind of acted like he was afraid of me. He began to get this distinct precautionary look on his face when he approached me to talk. He'd walk out of his way to avoid me or stand back when I would walk by. The lack of connection and attention left me feeling very brokenhearted, forsaken, and unlovable. I bought into the lie that I would never get to be loved until I never got angry again. Sometimes, that would feel like, never, even though I tried everything I knew to do to get free. In those moments, I would contemplate leaving the family, thinking they would be better off without me. That way, Phillip could find another wife who was slow to anger, soft-spoken, sweet, gentle, and nurturing to him and the children. Someone who would be a good example for my girls and love Phillip like he fantasized about being loved—someone who was everything that I was not. It was very lonely to live in a home where the people I loved most were frightened of me, except my Wilson.

The loneliness drove me outside my marriage and home to find love, acceptance, and belonging in Christian female friendships or Christian women's groups, like Bible studies or prayer meetings. *I caught you! You thought I was going to say something else didn't you, and my story was going get all juicy?* I found it so much easier to show up on my best behavior for a catch-up lunch date and impress my friend(s) with all the significant things I was doing, or for a prayer meeting and wow them with my spirituality, than to find love inside my marriage and family in the chaotic-mundane, day-to-day living with family who'd seen me at my worst, knew all my manipulation tactics, and were leery of me.

At the peak of my loneliness and neglect, a young man that we used to mentor at the church in South Georgia, came back into town. He was at a low spot in his life, looking for a new start with no place to start. In short, we discovered he'd been writing country songs that we thought had lots of potential. We told him if he got his partner to come to town, we would help them make a start in the music industry. Next thing I knew, these two young men were living in my house, drinking all my coffee, and my coffee cups started mysteriously disappearing. These two young bucks were not only talented, but nice looking, very charming, and convincing. For a little bit, I was kind of playing the role of their manager, getting them connected with country music folks in our community. They were always hugging me, teasing and flirting with me, telling me how awesome I was, and how nice looking I was for my age. I tried not to show it, but I was eating up all their attention and affection.

The guys started to gain some momentum with their music and looked like they might be on the edge of launching their dream as country artists. My friends and I would go to bars to hear them play and compete. The whole environment became very enticing and alluring. I began to fantasize about the duo hitting the big time and me remaining their manager. I could picture myself jetting around the country, playing gigs and concerts, and living the country and western music life, which in my head looked like me buying a pink jeep, getting tattoos, living in boots, drinking in bars, dancing on pool tables, and living a wild life. *Don't ask me where in the heck I got those ideas.*

I became obsessed with that fantasy, thinking about it day and night, until I could visualize myself justifiably leaving Phillip and the kids to run after this crazy life. What had gotten into me? I didn't know who I could talk to about all this that wouldn't judge me. Then, I thought of my old best friend in Tulsa. *Remember her?* Well, I called her and confessed everything. Just like I was deep down, secretly hoping she would do, she told me that the whole sorted plan was completely ridiculous. In great detail, she confronted me with how justifiably unreasonable my fantasy was. I was so grateful for her honesty and loving confrontation rattling me back to reality. That's what true friends are for.

My simple act of confession seemed to minimalize the whole fantastically stupid idea and I quickly snapped out of my obsession with it. Not even a month later, the guys busted up over money and women, so that would have busted up my fantasy anyway. What a relief to have the guys and all that I had attached to them, out of my house and out of my head. This little escapade with the country duo only served as a reprieve from the emotional wreckage of my marriage and family. It was there, faithfully waiting for me once I'd landed safely back onto the performance treadmill.

Christmas 2013 rolled around, which meant it was time for my annual Christmas card picture/letter. I rallied the family together to meet with a photographer after church for a "happy family" photo. I had learned over the years that if I caught them when they were already going to be getting dressed up for something, that it was less stressful than making an appointment to have our picture made and create this big moment for everyone to pose in front of a camera, looking picture perfect. I had also learned to chill out about the way everyone dressed. Instead of controlling what everyone wore or manipulating everyone into looking the way I wanted them to, I acquiesced to having the family democratically vote on a color scheme and allowing each member to choose their own outfit, only advice-giving when asked. This seemed to cut down on the tension that had typically escalated into a blow-out in the past, like the one for our 2011 Christmas photo. *That one left me gun shy.*

Thankfully, 2013 went as smoothly as it could possibly go, being that my crew was hungry for lunch. They got rewarded with a nice one at a restaurant for posing so well for the photographer; and all was well with us for the rest of the day, making for a peaceful Sunday. As for the update letter that I traditionally sent along with our annual Christmas photo card, well, one didn't get written that year. I could think of nothing impressive to say. Outside of the disgraceful antics I pulled with the country singing fellas, I could nowise see a thing through all my brain fog worth recounting. Moreover, after last year's outlandishly braggadocious news alert, I ashamedly vowed to never send another. So, breaking a twenty-one-year tradition, only a Christmas photo card got snail-mailed off to our friends and family far and wide. The rest were passively hand-delivered to local friends or passed out to our congregants. I distinctly remember standing in the doorway of our little white church, feeling like a hypocrite, wishing everyone a Merry Christmas as they left for the holidays and handing them our happy family Christmas photo card, which was only smoke and mirrors.

The new year only brought us more of the same calamity and chaos that we were accustomed to, but as fate would have it, 2014 brought with it much worse. It was as if the girls collaborated to act out all at the same time and go crazy-crazy on us, doing everything that scares a good parent to death. I thought to myself, I could react to this by having a complete mental breakdown and get locked away in a padded cell or I could run away. Running away sounded so much more fun. So, I conjured up a new twist on my get-way fantasy that looked like me escaping to the beach on a pink Harley, where no one knew me, getting tattoos, finding a waitress job at a beachfront restaurant by day, dancing at clubs at night, spending all my spare time melting on the sand in the sun, living wild and free.

Dealing with the girl's craziness and waiting for just the right moment to make my escape, I started binge eating to numb out. I started putting on more weight than I ever had before, which freaked me out because I never had a weight problem before. *Thank God, He doesn't give us more than we can handle!* I went to drive-throughs during the day when I was out "running errands" so I could numb out on junk food without anyone seeing. I wasn't being a bad influence on the kids and Phillip wasn't correcting my eating habits. If I hid it, then I didn't have to feel bad about it. Right?

Finally, I was feeling so much shame, emotion, torment, and misery that I just couldn't keep it all in for another second. I had to get it all out, in a safe place. I just couldn't hide any longer. So, I fibbed to Phillip that I was going to a prayer meeting with my Bible study group from church, just to get out away by myself. It wasn't a total lie because I was going to a prayer meeting, but just with Jesus in the parking lot of our neighborhood clubhouse, where I scream-prayed and ugly-cried to Jesus until I had no voice or tears left, emptying out all the shame and emotions. When I got home, Phillip was engrossed in his nightly numbing-out routine in front of the T.V., halfway through a bag of family-sized tortilla chips. I discreetly went upstairs, quickly went through my nighttime routine, slipped in bed, and turned out the lights before anyone got a glimpse of my red puffy eyes.

The following night, after dinner and all the girls had tightly locked themselves behind their bedroom doors and little Wilson was doing his bedtime routine, Phillip said he wanted to talk with me in his office. Getting called into his office meant you were in trouble and about to hear a Popeye, I've-had-all-I-can-stands speech. I immediately broke into a nervous sweat. I timidly sauntered in and sat down, as he rolled his office chair right in front of me, uncomfortably close. He proceeded to tell me that the Lord had told him that he needed to set me free to do what made me happy. *I about fell out of my chair, folks.* You would have thought that he'd been a fly on the wall of my car the night before, overhearing my screaming prayers and ugly crying.

Genuinely shocked at what just came out of his mouth, I asked, "Are you joking?"

With his chin leaning on his fist, he shook his head, no.

Then, I suspiciously inquired, "Did I accidentally record myself last night praying in my car and somehow you heard it?"

He gave me an "I-don't-know-what-you're-talking-about look" in response. I knew right then and there that this was a set-up from the Lord.

I burst like a backed-up sewage pipe, crap flying everywhere. I confessed the fantasizing, the insane idea of running off to the beach, the tattoos, the pink vehicles, living wild, everything—major unclogging. I explained how I didn't understand why this was happening, that all I could figure was either I was going mentally bonkers or having a mid-life, menopausal breakdown. As I sobbed with my face in my hands, Phillip reached over and hugged me. I couldn't remember the last time he touched me. It felt like a warm blanket that I could have stayed wrapped in for eternity, it felt too wonderful.

As he pulled back into his chair, he gently replied, "I believe this is your mind and body telling you that you need a life change because you are burned out."

As I gave him a puppy-like, ear-raised head tilt, in wide-eyed wonderment, he proceeded to share his solution for me, which went something like this, "I think you should put the kids back in school next year and find a job doing something that you love."

I had to put my finger in my ear and jiggle it a little to make sure there wasn't anything blocking my hearing. So, he repeated himself. I was dumbfounded and speechless. Then he stood, laid his hand on my head that again felt warm and comforting, and prayed for me. It felt like the hands of mercy. As he walked out of his office, he told me to let him know what I decided to do. Who was that Masked Marauder, that just swept me away with his words, his hug, his prayer, and his plan? I sat in astonishment with my mouth hanging open for what seemed several minutes, unable to move, pondering what he'd said, and what it might look like to enroll the girls back in school and go do what made me happy. I hadn't thought about that in so long, I didn't know where to start, mainly because I didn't know where my role as a homemaker ended and where the rest of me began.

Well, I didn›t take off to the beach, even though it did make me happy. In fact, I didn't have to go looking at all. A job landed right in my lap. One of my good friends, who was a barre instructor, asked if I'd like to work part-time at the check-in desk at a private barre studio where she worked, just 10 minutes from my house. I couldn't have thought of a more perfect way to get my feet wet back in the working world. I said, "Yes!" to her fun job offer.

After few months excelling at that, I felt ready for a bigger and better job. I knew exactly what that would be, as I had taken that time to contemplate what I felt would really make me happy. It turned out to be fashion, which, of course, made total sense, as my claim to fame was "Best Dressed." I had to overcome a lot of shame as an older, stay-at-home mom venturing back in the workforce. I discovered there was a stigma to overcome that I could actually be valuable in the workplace again. After three attempts at it, I landed an assistant manager position at a *Charming Charlie,* because the store manager was looking for someone more mature (a politically correct way of calling someone old these days). Well, lucky me, I was "mature."

However, it didn't take long for me to struggle to bring home any money because I spent so much of it on the irresistible accessories, which became like an out-of-control-addiction. The brain fog, forgetfulness, and focus issues caused me to show up as a big, incompetent ditz, and feel inadequate for the job. My feet hurt so bad from standing on concrete nine hours a day, it left me wanting to do nothing but lay and watch episodes of "Once Upon a Time" when I was at home, which, in turn, made me feel worthless around the house. The injustice I saw and experienced from the store manager, coupled with all the other negativity, made me crazy. I felt no other option but to quit, leaving me humiliated and feeling like an epic failure. That job didn't make me happy one bit, it only made things worse.

Phillip seemed utterly disappointed with me, throwing his hands in the air and shouting, "I don't know what's going to make you happy, woman!"

The impact of his words hit my soul like a semi-truck that had lost its brakes. I wanted to crawl under a rock and die. No matter what I did to improve myself, striving to become his fantasy, it was never enough to get him to love me. Trying to prove my worth ended in epic failure, just like that job. I felt disappointment cloak over me like heavy, gooey tar that weighed me down, causing the movement of my life to seem heavy and in slow motion. It drained all the life out of me, leaving me feeling like a dead battery. I didn't know what was wrong with me and didn't know how to get better. I felt hopeless. I didn't feel like taking my life like I used to when I struggled with suicidal depression, but I certainly didn't feel like I deserved to be alive.

Our 2014 Christmas photo card was not a happy family group picture. None of us could even stand to be in the same vicinity together long enough to take a photo together. I didn't have the fortitude to rally the family together for a picture-perfect moment. Of course, Phillip and I had put on so much weight from our emotional, binge-eating habits that we only wanted to be pictured from the neck up. I managed to pull together a collage of individual shots of me, Phillip, and each of our girls, attempting, in our best efforts, to look like something of worth. Little Wilson and our doggies looked oblivious, cute, and happy. I was not at all excited about mailing it or handing it out to anyone, but I couldn't bring myself to break tradition all together. I had to somehow let the folks in our world know that we were still the perfect family. No one could know we were falling apart on the inside.

> **Little did I know I was still holding true
> to the pervading lie from my childhoodthat was
> lying way down there in the depths of my soul.**

It was covered up by all the hard years, words faded and hard to see, but it hadn't moved from its coveted spot, and it still read like this, "It would be more honorable to die than to be found out."

Phillip

I remember a turning point for me in the middle of Darlena's struggles with our kids. My oldest daughter was on a prodigal journey. What would you do if you knew your beautiful daughter was being taken advantage of by a young punk? Here's what happened.

I was sitting in my truck on a school night waiting for my daughter to get off work. It was almost quitting time at the local chicken sand-wich joint. Her shift was ending very soon which meant my daughter was facing one of the most important decisions of her life. She could either jump in my truck and gone straight home from work or she could protest my authority and hop in the truck of a local want-to-be-thug.

He was a dropout who snuck into her life like a snake sneaks into a garden. He offered her what she wanted; a fun time, but his real goal was a one-night stand that would leave her defiled.

This was not my first rodeo with an adolescent knucklehead. I was schooled by some of the best players in my high school years. I knew how to scare this kid off with fatherly intimidation. I sat there for fifteen minutes after he pulled up to the store. I debated in my head, "Do I run him off or do I let her choose?" The clock was ticking in my ear and my heart rate was rising. There were visions of me raging on this kid, flashing like a bad YouTube video. Pastor beats up daughter's boyfriend in the parking lot. What do I do? Prayer started to fall out of my mouth. The only spiritual thought I had was to lay my hands on this boy, not for prayer, but for vindication.

"Lord, what do you want me to do?" Silence. "Lord, please show me what to do." Silence. "I can't do the right thing because I'm so angry, Lord, please help me." Then this phrase popped into my head. Let her choose. She will never know true love until she chooses. All of a sudden, I felt empowered. The choice was hers. I know it sounds like an irresponsible move as a parent, but I had battled her for years over boy issues.

She came bobbing out the door with a super happy look on her face like she was about to ride a merry-go-round. Yes, she jumped into his truck which was running and ready. They backed up and took off down the road. My head dropped. I couldn't believe I had prayed, and God didn't intervene. Why? Why isn't God helping me? Why is she doing this to me? Tears streamed down my face. I had failed as a father. This was one of the lowest moments of my life.

My drive home was hell. What was I going to tell Darlena? I walked in the door and my wife already knew this was a possibility. Once again, there was a female power struggle that ended in another massive mess. My daughter was seeing this dude and my wife was trying to stop it. My daughter rebelled against the mandate and ran away with the guy. This was one of many battles we lost with this child.

The next day, we called the police to file the runaway report. They picked her up and brought her back to the house. I couldn't believe the hate that spouted from her mouth. She spent the night sowing her wild oats and we were the most awful parents on the earth.

Twenty-four hours later, I was staring at the congregation. I should have a meticulously prepared sermon ready for eager parishioners. But I couldn't get it done. My night was filled with anxious pacing back and forth, worrying about my daughter and my wife who usually collapsed under stress like this. I fumbled with the microphone and looked down for a minute hoping to waste some time.

The words that spilled out of my mouth surprised me, "I don't have a sermon for you, I have a prayer request."

I gained some confidence with the first line, "My daughter is on a prodigal journey and I have not slept in two days. I know that I'm your pastor, but my wife and I are in a lot of pain right now."

The crowd sat forward on the edge of their seats, "I know I should know what to do, but I don't know how to handle this moment."

I tried to involve others, "Maybe you came here today with a big need that you are worried about and you could use some prayer."

Some people were crying, some were shocked, and others didn't know what to do. Authenticity in a church service is rare, but that morning, I vulnerably revealed our real needs as a family. I felt a ten-ton weight drop off my shoulders. This didn't stop my daughter's rebellion, but it set something in motion for Darlena and I. For the first time, we found allies who knew the truth about our situation.

Summary

Money, status, and things did not bring us happiness. Buying the nice house, getting good jobs, having more money, and finding the best schools for our kids did not improve our marriage. We turned the pursuit of stuff into a quest for certainty and security. The trouble is that our pursuit of the American dream/fantasy put us back on the performance treadmill. The performance was about looking good in public and hiding our real problems behind closed doors. Old lies crept back into our hearts. That opened us up to bad habits that increased our shame on a personal level and broadened our disconnection as a couple.

When you're not winning outside your home and that job or whatever position, in Darlena's case as a homeschool mom, you try to overcompensate for inside your home. It will show up by trying to get your spouse and/or children to make you feel good about yourself. This could look like manipulating for compliments or demanding respect, then punishing them with your emotions for not making you feel a certain way, treating the people you love and trust in ways that you would not even consider treating others outside your home.

The turning point came when I threw caution to the wind and revealed our struggles to the world around us. The radical shift away from hiding and performing was a desperate attempt to find a breakthrough for my marriage and family. Healing relationships required me to practice courage. I believe it saved my daughter's life and began the healing process for our marriage and family.

Have you found yourself performing to hide what is really going on in your life?

How has that been working out for you?

Have you attempted to find value and worth that you can't get outside your home from your husband and/or kids?

How does public performance hide the real you?

Chapter 11

BECOMING COURAGEOUS & COMING OUT OF HIDING

My desperation left me to do the only thing I knew to do when staring in the face of hopelessness. I desperately cried out in the middle of my bleak, dark Wasteland to the Savior, I couldn't see or feel in my godforsaken state, but that I, ever so remotely, believed in from somewhere deep in my gut. He was still there. He was still watching, listening, and waiting. I feebly attempted to form prayers that sounded more like a dying person's lifeless last words, which interestingly had a familiar ring to them from maybe somewhere in my past. Oh yes, thirteen years ago, when we lived in Tulsa, Oklahoma, and I thought Phillip was dying of Hepatitis-B and I wanted to die to from life-sucking, depression. I whispered prayers of quiet desperation like these. At that time, my prayers were pleas to be spared of physical death that seemed to have us pinned in. This time, I was petitioning Heaven to bring me back to life because I felt dead on the inside.

Sometimes, life seems daunting and frightening when it feels so out of control or that it's slipping away. If you've ever found yourself at such an impasse, you would understand that the only appeal that can be mustered up in your frailness sounds inept, "Jesus, help me."

I believe this measly, little cry for mercy holds as much weight, if not more, than grand, reverent, audacious invocations.

Those three small words communicate the earnest belief that I have reached the end of myself or the end of my rope. These kinds of prayers resound imploringly off the walls of heaven entreating the angel armies to deploy their rescue units. Heaven's response is, "Perfect. Now, we can FINALLY help them." The angels on assignment began to come for me, for us…on a divine rescue mission from God.

My first angel on assignment was Barb, an acquaintance of mine, who just showed up one Sunday at our church, for no apparent reason. At the end of worship, Phillip stepped to the front of the sanctuary, took the mic like he did every Sunday, and said, "Turn around and greet your neighbors."

When I turned around, there she stood. It took me by surprise because there was no reason for her to be at our church. She had a church home and we had no special speaker that day to motivate her to come. After our greeting and idol chit-chat, I asked her why she was there, and she appeared uneasy. She nervously explained how she was halfway to her church that morning when she heard the Holy Spirit say she was supposed to go to our church that morning. So, she obeyed the Lord and turned her car in the opposite direction. As she drove, she prayed and asked the Holy Spirit what she was going to our church for. She sensed the Lord telling her that I needed help.

I was very curious at this point and could tell from her humble demeanor that her story was legitimate. She asked if there was somewhere more private that we could talk and possibly pray. I led her downstairs to a storeroom in the basement of the church across from the nursery. She inquired how I was doing. It was very apparent to me the Lord had sent her, so I didn't hold back telling her. As soon as I finished sharing, she laid her hand on my forehead and began praying. Her hand felt warm and loving, like Phillip's had, an extension of mercy, once more. As she diligently prayed, I wanted so badly to feel something; to feel God again, to feel alive again. She was praying so intensely that she was shaking and perspiring, but I didn't feel a thing except guilt for not receiving as intensely as she was prayed. I thought I owed it to her to at least feel better because of how she'd availed herself to me and obeyed the Lord that morning. I graciously thanked her and she left.

She showed back up the next Sunday and said, "He told me to come back again. So, here I am."

We both laughed awkwardly and headed back to the storage room to pray. She laid her hands, one on each of my shoulders. As she prayed, I felt electrical pulses going down through my shoulders from her hands. It was quite cool. It was as if I was getting my battery charged or something. She prayed for me for the duration of the church service. By the end of her prayers, I felt what seemed like electrical surge throughout my entire body, as if I were being brought back to life. I was awestruck because it felt so awesome and exhilarating. I didn't know what to even think. I was so energized from those prayers I think I could have taken off out the backdoor of the church and run all the way home.

She came back a third Sunday and it became comical at this point. When I turned around to greet my neighbors, there stood Barb, in the back of the sanctuary, waving at me with a quirky grin. This time we went to the youth room, since they weren't there, so we could have more room, in case things got electric again. She told me this time that the Lord told her to keep coming to pray for me until I felt completely back to normal. Wow, I found that hard to believe, but okay. She started with her hand on my forehead again, then her hand started to shake so that it had my bangs sticking straight up in the air.

She paused and stepped back to look me in the eyes and said, "I just heard the Lord say that your brain is exhausted," to which I responded, "That sounds about right."

So, she got behind me, land both her hands on the back of my head and started back with the fierce prayers of healing for my brain.

Then, I kid you not, the next thing that happened felt like a lightning bolt had struck me on top of the head, shot down through my body, and out my fingers and toes. But it didn't stop there. It just kept on so that I couldn't remain standing. My knees gave way and I crumpled to the floor. The lightning strike didn't stop when I hit the floor, but switched to surging through my chest, like some defibrillator on steroids. I was dribbling around on the floor like a basketball, as this powerful force was ripping through my body. Of course, Barb was trying to keep her hands on me as she continued to pray ferociously, so she was bouncing all around, too. I had no concept of time while all this was taking place. It wasn't painful in a bad way, but painful in the best way, like the saying, "it hurts so good." Nonetheless, I eventually couldn't handle it any longer, yet never wanted it to stop. It was wild and wonderful! If you could have seen me, you probably would have thought I was having convulsions on the floor, but that's not how I felt when I got up off the floor. I was wringing wet with sweat, breathing like I'd just finished high-impact aerobics, and my hair looked like a hornet's nest, but I felt alive again, and that's all that mattered to me in the moment. My brain felt lighter, if that makes any sense to you, and like it was firing on all cylinders once again. It was miraculous. I was stupefied, to say the least.

When I'd gotten ahold of myself and calmed down, Barb shared how it had dawned on her the past week how much my story sounded like what her husband had struggled with in recent years. She told me how she had to convince him to go to a doctor with his symptoms, which sounded like mine, and he was diagnosed with ADD. He didn't want traditional medication, so they prayed to discover a natural alternative. After a few days of praying, a lady came knocking at their door whose car had broken down in front of their house. They invited her in to use the phone and wait for a tow truck. They made small talk with her to discover that her son had ADD and she'd traveled the world researching the causes natural cures for ADD. Her latest finding was a pharmaceutical-grade amino acid that changed her son's life. They, in turn, shared the husband's story and told her that she'd been an answer to their prayers. Barbara's husband started taking the supplement and it completely changed his life as well.

So, Barb became convinced over the past week that she'd been sent by God to share it with me, too. Knowing we were struggling financially and without insurance, she offered to pay for my initial doctor's visit and my first month's supply. I typically wasn't one to accept help, but to refuse her would feel like refusing God, who'd obviously orchestrated this entire rescue mission. She took me to a walk-in clinic right then, got the prescription filled, and I took one right away. Within thirty minutes of taking it, I felt the heavy fog that weighed my brain down, dissipate. It was amazing. Barbara concluded her mission had been accomplished. She drove me home. I didn't even know how to thank her. *I mean, who does this kind of thing for someone she barely knows?* I was deeply humbled by the entire experience and beyond grateful to have my brain back. I still take that supplement, to this day.

Next, a rescue plane took Phillip and I to Branson, Missouri, for a Marriage Intensive at the Focus on the Family Retreat Center that the church board graciously agreed to pay for. I can't give you the play-by-play of those four days because I don't remember many details, which is unlike me. Mainly due to the fact that I was too focused on keeping my duke's up, so if at any point during our stay I needed to defend myself, I wouldn't be caught off guard. You see, although Phillip didn't come right out and say it, I knew in my bones he signed us up for that thing in hopes that someone would fix me and my anger/rage problem

For some reason, I really enjoy taking those kinds of tests and evaluations that help you discover stuff about yourself or figure out why you do what you do. Well, we took one that I'd never heard of before that helped us understand how our fear triggers kept us stuck in that crazy cycle of arguing anytime we tried to have a conversation. That was extremely insightful and helpful, and we got to bring home a big poster with our crazy cycle drawn on it to hang up on our bedroom wall and remind us of our crazy fears every day, like a souvenir. But in all seriousness, Phillip having his huge breakthrough about me not being the problem in our marriage was the game-changer for us. I think for the first time in our entire marriage, he saw himself as a contributor to our problems, and actually felt compassion for me as the target of his blame.

Although I saw myself as the reason for our problems as well, it helped me see how I had some blaming of my own to deal with, that I was not aware of. He blamed me for my anger/rage issues, but I blamed him for not loving me the way I needed to be loved. When we stopped blaming each other and realized we both were responsible for the lost years and the devastation, it took so much pressure off of our marriage and tension out of our home. That felt so refreshing, like a cool breeze blowing through our house that brought hope for life and love to bloom there again. Now, we could back away from working on our relationship that was getting us nowhere fast and work on the things in our own hearts and souls causing us to remain gridlocked in our marriage.

My mental issues had greatly improved and our marriage had progressed a little, but something big, dark, and heavy lurked in my soul. My best attempt to describe it is that it was like a loathsome feeling of valuelessness. I also still felt very disconnected from God, still unable to see Him, hear Him, or feel Him in the Spirit. All I could hear from the unseen realm was a tormenting voice in my head, mocking me day and night, incessantly reminding me in a nasty, sinister tone, "Your life is a joke." The mocking was making feel crazy, yet I believed it to be true. With everyone I met, I told impressive stories about my past, about what once was and who I used to be. I felt like a has-been that lived in the afterglow of past fame, which had become dull and worn out from overuse. If I got really honest with myself, Best Dressed nominee and T.V. Talk Show guest weren't really even that big of a deal in the first place. My glory days were over and I was all washed up.

Around this time, Phillip sensed the Lord urging him to step down from the lead pastor role with the church and get our own ministry back up and running again. *Remember Get Real Ministries?* This brought a lot of relief for me, as the lens of the microscope zoomed out some. We were offered a great new office space with plenty of room to hold group events and Phillip was excited about it. He also told me that he wanted me by his side now that I wasn't home with kids anymore. I thought to myself, "That is really sweet, but I really don't think I have anything to offer anyone anymore."

We had an open house to advertise the opening of our new office and offered to pray for anyone who wanted prayer. I froze up, like I used to when I walked in the homeschool coop. I was just standing there sweating, afraid to pray for anyone, so I just followed behind Phillip as he laid hands on folks and prayed. I felt so useless. I could hear Jeff Probst, the host of Survivor, in my mind, when he was telling the losers to go back to camp, "Got nothin' for ya!" I panicked at the thought of spending the rest of my days feeling like this. *Afraid to pray for people and can't hear from God. How pitiful and embarrassing.*

"I can't live like this!" I screamed inside my head. God either needs to deliver me or take me home. These thoughts sounded all too familiar, from my Tulsa days, right before we drove to that little church in South Georgia. I was willing to go through all the peaks and valleys I had gone through before just to be close to Him again.

The open house took place on a Thursday night. The next day at home, while everyone was gone, I spent hours listening to worship music, bawling, pleading, and sending up prayers to Heaven that sounded more like, S.O.S distress signals, in hopes that maybe one would get heard and an emergency response team would be sent for me. I'm reminded of the lyric from Lauren Daigle's song, *Rescue*: "I hear you whisper underneath your breath. I hear your S.O.S. I will send out an army to find you in the middle of your darkest night. It's true, I will rescue you."

And He did. The Holy Spirit revealed another rescue mission the next morning.

When I woke on Saturday morning, I felt awful from crying so much the day before. My head was pounding, my eyes were puffy and red, my nose was still stuffy, and I had cotton mouth. I dragged myself out of bed and into the bathroom. As I stood gazing at my post-catharsis face, I heard the Lord speak for the first time in three years. I was surprised to hear His voice, but even more astonished at what He had to say to me, "Go to the Hollywood church's school of ministry and I will refresh you, restore you, renew you, and reposition you in ministry." *Are you kidding me? I didn't hear from Him in three years and the first thing He has to say to me is go to the last church on the planet that I would ever want to go to?* As elated and relieved to finally hear His voice again and humbled that He had gone to all the trouble to think up a rescue plan, I was like, "Good morning, Lord! It's really great to hear from You and all. But, no thanks, I can't do that." *And I had good reasons!* I did not have the money or the time. I wouldn't even think about going by myself. I had too much dignity to go back to that Hollywood church that got us to move halfway across the nation just to ditch us after we got here (with sass and a Z-formation). *So, there.*

I did not say a word to Phillip about my little encounter with the Lord in the bathroom that morning, but a series of events led me to tell Phillip the whole story that night. I just knew he would agree with me that it would be impossible for me to go. You know what he did? Pulled out his cell phone and texted the pastor of the Hollywood church and told him the story. Of course, he and Phillip had already made up, but I, obviously, still had an issue that I needed to deal with.

The pastor's response was, "Great! We'd love to have her. Orientation starts in the morning. I'll tell the director to expect her."

Can you believe it? God had set me up so I wouldn't have time to change my mind and back out. I figured God, Phillip, and the Hollywood pastor were all in cahoots. I woke up as nervous as heck, but ate humble pie for breakfast, sucked up my pride, and headed out the door for ministry school orientation, as Phillip waved and hollered,

"Have fun!" with a snarky grin on his face. When I arrived, I was greeted with hugs and, "We're so glad you're here!" like nothing had ever happened. I had a sneaking feeling I had made the right choice.

I could not have conjured up in my wildest dreams where my yes would take me that school year. The first night of class, I heard the Lord speak to Lord, again. I sensed He wanted me to understand the focus of the coming year would be a divine romance between He and I; my job was just to sit back and receive. That seemed like a foreign concept, but I obeyed as best I knew how. That instruction came with Psalm 23, which I read from my Message Bible:

A David Psalm

God, my shepherd!
I don't need a thing.
You have bedded me down in lush meadows,
you find me quiet pools to drink from.
True to your word,
you let me catch my breath
and send me in the right direction.
Even when the way goes through
Death Valley,
I'm not afraid
when you walk at my side.
Your trusty shepherd's crook
makes me feel secure.
You serve me a six-course dinner
right in front of my enemies.
You revive my drooping head;

my cup brims with blessing.
Your beauty and love chase after me
every day of my life.
I'm back home in the house of God
for the rest of my life.

I couldn't conceive what this meant, as sitting and receiving wasn't my M.O. But I agreed to do the best I knew how. My next instruction was to **not** seek after anything I had ever had before, because He had something more for me that was far greater than I had ever known. As you have probably gathered from my story, I had already had a rather amazing journey with the Lord, so it was difficult to fathom anything beyond what I had already experienced. Again, I agreed to not have an agenda. So, when I showed up for school each night, I just held my heart and hands in a posture to receive.

About three months into the school year, I had an off-the-chain, supernatural encounter with God's love, at home in my bedroom, unlike anything I had ever known. It was an uncommon and unfathomable, wild and wonderful encounter with God that I find hard to put into words. Here's my feeble attempt to put a two hour, extraordinarily intentional, yet heavenly experience in a few words.

Initially, an intoxicating joy started to fill up my whole insides with bubbly joy and bliss, like warm fuzzies on steroids. Then it was as if my bedroom began to be overtaken by a thick, heavy, tangible presence that became so weighty, I could no longer stand under the weight of it. So, I laid down on my bed. This weighty presence began bearing down on my entire body so forcefully that I could not move. While lying under the weight of it, I thought to myself, "What is this?

What is happening to me? What if I can't handle it and I'm not able to breathe?"

Just before fear took over and I started to panic, I heard these words, "This is the rest that comes from knowing the depths of My love. It has come to press out everything that doesn't belong to you and doesn't belong in My Kingdom."

Once I heard the comforting voice of my Heavenly Father, I just surrendered to the pressure, letting His presence overtake me and do the work He had come to do in my soul. Wow, pressing out everything that doesn't belong to me or Him. How could I be afraid of that?

This experience lasted for close to two hours. I believe it goes without saying, that I had an extraordinary, life-altering moment of impact with the Savior. I'll save the details for another time and place. However, I will declare this: Creation was made, in all its wonder and awe, to give us a glimpse of what God's love has the capability to do when surrendered to. He's not so high and mighty in the sky that He's unwilling to bend down low and unleash His power on our tiny, minuscule, underserving lives, to shoo away our monsters and outshine our darkest night. That's what good Fathers do."

One morning in the presence of my Heavenly Father altered the trajectory of my life up to that point, turning a lifetime of unloving into a well of love overflowing. This supernatural encounter with the love of God had the power to change the way I saw myself, my life, and how I saw Phillip and our marriage in an instant. Something I got such a kick out of was that it spilled over onto everyone that came into contact with me, like I was contagious, for about nine months. Phillip posted on Facebook that revival had hit our house. I loved this, because not a soul was in my bedroom that day, to experience what I felt or witness what was happening. The average Christian would find it hard to believe, hearing such a whopping story about encountering the love of God in such a way. I might have found it a bit fantastical, just hearing someone tell such a story.

So, Phillip booked speaking engagements all around our community, in churches, women's groups, and Bible studies to share the testimony of my Divine Love Encounter. What he witnessed happening in me, he thought was too profound to not share it with anyone who was willing to hear. Getting to do that was so amazing, because each time I shared, without fail, an intoxicating presence would fill the room that felt heavy and warm. Then no one would want to move or could move, nor did they want the experience to end.

I loved that I could give away my encounter and that it wasn't some special experience just for me. It was for anyone who wanted it.

Every amazing change or shift that came later, I connect back to this one amazing morning I encountered His deep-as-the-ocean kind of love, and I have never been the same. Every time I say those words, it reminds me of Kim Walker-Smith of Jesus Culture, singing, "He Loves Us," live on the We Cry Out CD. She pauses toward the end of the song and says:

> "His presence, His love is so thick and tangible in this room tonight. And there are some of you who've never encountered the love of God. Tonight, God wants to encounter you. He wants you to feel His amazing love. Without it, these are just songs, these are just words, these are just instruments. Without it, it's like we are

just up here making noise. The love of God changes us and we are never the same after we encounter the love of God. And right now, if you've never encountered the love of God, and you would know because you would never be the same! You're never the same after you encounter the love of God! You'd know cause you'd never be the same after you'd encountered the love of God. So, brace yourself, cause He's about to blow in this place! You're about to encounter the love of God!"

I felt puzzled by the kind of love that Kim was referring to the first time I heard the song back in 2007. I thought that I had experienced the love of God, but she made it sound like I was missing out on something. Well, I was. I can most assuredly testify to knowing that kind of love now. It's the kind of encounter that suddenly switches on a lightbulb inside your head and solidifies your identity as a son or daughter of the King of kings. You finally understand that you deserve to feel this way because it's your birthright as a child of God.

After that morning, my heart and soul became soft, raw, and pliable; ready for a speedy recovery and easy repair. My unforeseen rendezvous helped me recover the part of me that was capable and courageous—the greatheartedness I had first found in the campground at Pleasant Valley. This is the part of me that I would need to restore the wreckage of my marriage, which I had sacrificed on the altar of perfection. I would need it to bravely accomplish the next rescue mission, as there was more soul work yet to be done.

At the end of the school year, to continue the momentum of breakthrough in our marriage and our quest for soul healing, Phillip and

I participated in Dr. Caroline Leaf's, *21-Day Brain Detox*, together. For twenty-one days in a row, we went on our cute and quaint front porch with our breakfast and hot tea. *Now don't lower our coolness rating because we're not coffee drinkers, people.* This was a sweet bonding time for us that we shared together in the morning before the kids and dogs were rustling around. I coincidentally was reading, *Daring Greatly*, by Brené Brown. During those twenty-one days, in May of 2016, I had the most profound light-bulb moments about myself as I was reading about the effects of shame and focus on targeting lies. It hit me so hard, it left me breathless. Big moments have a tendency to do that to me. It was a moment of impact that left me never the same. Phillip and I were sitting on the front porch doing our 21-day Detox steps together, when I received an incredible revelation from the Lord. He said that I had experienced that three-year dark night of the soul because I was exhausted with hiding in the shame of my closet rage.

On June 8, 2016, I was scheduled to share my testimony before an audience of 300 plus people at Pinewood Studios, Fayetteville, Georgia. The Lord challenged me to use this platform to confess this and what had been tormenting me for over twenty years. It seemed my challenge needed to match the level of torment that I had been living in for so many years, so I could finally be free. As crazy and scary as it sounded, I believed the Lord had led me to the precipice where there could be no turning back from coming out of hiding. Although the thought of it made me feel a little faint, I was willing to take the risk to free this person on the inside that fiercely ached to be free.

So, I made it to the big day. I was approaching the point in my testimony where I was about to do the big reveal. I thought I might lose my breath and die right there on the spot. Instead, before the confession rolled off my tongue, I set the stage with these words, "The issue that I've been hiding in shame for over twenty years as a minister's wife is a…" and I turned my head to the left, away from the mic, gasped for air, as my heart was pounding so hard that it was difficult to breathe and I thought surely I'd pass out right there in front of the whole crowd staring at me. *Lord, don't fail me now!* Then I turned back to the crowd.

As my eyes panned the room in what seemed like slow-motion, I looked right into the faces of strangers, the faces of special friends I had invited, the faces of important people from our community I had not expected, and the endearing eyes of my sweet husband sitting on the front row pulling for me so hard that his forehead glistened with perspiration. So, in front of God and everybody, I choked out, "…a tormenting battle with rage." Yep, I said it. Rage. And I didn't die, obviously. I could see the look of shock on some faces. So, I gave people a minute to take it all in. Since no one cast any stones, I bravely continued.

When I'd finished my testimony and wrapped up with a closing prayer, I was received with a standing ovation. A young lady, whom I'd never met, stood up abruptly, ran to the front and bear-hugged me.

She leaned over in the mic and said, "Because of what this woman has just shared, I believe a movement of vulnerability has been released in the body of Christ."

There was a priceless reward lying on the other side of that risk that day. I was completely liberated from a life of rage. I no longer have to live with it lurking in my gut, like a volcano waiting to erupt every waking moment. I was also honorably discharged from a life of hiding in shame, freed to live seen and known; not because I'd become perfect, but because I was perfectly loved.

Well, folks, that was the product of a serious undercover rescue mission that came in the form of an ocean liner from Heaven. Phillip?

It came for him, too. We just had some work we needed to do on ourselves before we could get back to the business of working on repairing our marriage. He was picked up a year later, went on his own personal cruise through the Hollywood School of Ministry, and had his own coming out of hiding party, which is his story to tell.

As for your rescue mission, maybe you've never known a God that chases you down and tackles you with His love, but He's always been chasing after you. He's been in hot pursuit of you to put the pieces of your heart and your marriage back together. You can know that kind of love in your marriage. If you let Him find you in the middle of your mess, He will rescue you from your Wasteland and guide you safely to the shores of your Dreamland. Nothing is too messy, too big, or too complicated that Jesus can't unravel, recover, and restore it with His "fierce" love. Chris Quilala, of Jesus Culture, sings a song called, *Fierce*, which I love because it testifies of how powerful the love of God is. Here's the best part:

"Like a tidal wave
Crashing over me
Rushing in to meet me here
Your love is fierce
That I can't escape
Tearing through the atmosphere

You surround me
You chase me down
You seek me out
How can I be lost when you have called me found...?"

All you have to do is step out of your hiding place and let Him catch you. Let His love lure you out of hiding—a life hidden by the shame of imperfection and a failing marriage. His love is powerful enough to break down the walls you've been hiding behind and press out all the things in your soul that have held you captive, kept you running on the treadmill of performance, and hopelessly stuck in your wasteland. He's calling, "Ollie, ollie, in come free!" Go on now, friends. Be brave. Run for base!

Phillip

I had prayed for this moment for over twenty years. Finally, somebody would be able to help us fix our marriage. I found the best marriage program on the planet. The organization was known for a 90 percent success rate. I thought to myself, *It better work because it cost me over $5,000 big ones to pay for this four-day intensive counseling experience.* This was a big chunk of our annual budget. We didn't spend money like this. Most of our one-week family vacations were spent camping in an RV.

For years, I felt like Darlena's irritable emotional syndrome was the core problem for our marriage. I took responsibility for little things like being impatient, raising my voice, and pulling away when I couldn't take it anymore. If you looked at the weight of the problem on an old double pan balancing scale, then, I would have a couple of bb's on my side and hers would have this ten-ton brass weight causing the scale to tip on her side. Guys, she was the problem. I knew it, she knew it, and I made sure the kids knew it.

We are sitting in this all-day counseling experience with four other couples. I intently listened to the other guys talk about their wives.

When it was my turn, I poured out my heart about what it was like to live with a rage-acholic. I made my case referring to the pain I suffered in my childhood from my abusive father and now I was enduring the tantrums of my wife. It felt like I was begging the judge to deliver me from my captor.

The counselor's unpredictable response blew my mind. He appeared to totally empathize with me. I thought he was on my side. His question pierced my soul like a surgeon's scalpel.

He gently asked, "What kind of man do you want to be when she gets angry?"

I stuttered a little and softly replied, "I want to be a part of the solution, not the problem."

He pressed, "Do you know why she gets angry?"

"Certainly," I popped back at him. "She uses anger to control me and get what she wants. She uses anger to overpower me and make me give up."

He looked at Darlena and pitched the question, "Why do you get angry?"

She said with tears running down her cheeks, "because I feel overwhelmed. I feel unloved because I can't live up to my husband's expectations. I get angry because I can't do everything by myself. I get angry when I am exhausted and feel like I am losing control of my life."

Wow! This was the turning point for me. This experience empowered me as a husband. Her anger was not an attack against me, but a deep struggle to please me that created torment. She wasn't a wench throwing a hissy fit and cracking her whip to put me in my place. Darlena was not trying to dominate our relationship, she was fighting to survive. Understanding her plight gave me compassion for her. I could see how desperately trying to be the perfect wife and to raise perfect kids was eating her up. The light switched on and my thinking totally flipped. I got it. She's not my enemy. She was laboring to get it right and to live up to my unrealistic expectations, but it was wearing her out.

Empathy for my wife filled my heart. I could see how hard she was trying to please me. I took the target off her back. For the first time in our marriage, I stopped blaming her for most of our problems. I learned something that day that transformed my heart towards my wife. I was expecting her to be my fantasy wife, the wife who didn't emotionally overreact, who never got angry, who always had a righteous spiritual attitude. I was expecting her to be a perfect wife which would make me feel like the perfect husband.

The compassion that God gave me for my wife that day turned into acceptance. I truly believe once I repented for being a controlling pharisee, she was freed up to change. Grace works the same way.

**God accepts us and then He empowers us
to become the people we long to be
from the strength of His acceptance.**

Summary

Once again, Darlena's need led us to discover something we both needed in our marriage. Although I judged her for her weaknesses, it was her vulnerabilities that lead to our biggest breakthroughs. The humility that she demonstrated inspired me to work on myself.

The big revelation about being responsible for our own fears and reactions was huge. She had the fear of being unloved because she never got it right and I had the fear of being powerless and incapable of helping her because she was too volatile. Neither of us felt loved. Fear was creating a disconnection.

I put too much pressure on Darlena to become the perfect woman which included less emotional reactions. Realizing that she was desperately trying to satisfy me caused me to have compassion for her struggle with anger. Empathy for one another's struggles was the catalyst for change. We learned if you want your spouse to grow and change then learn to empathize with them.

The foundation for healing a marriage starts with two people who are willing to take full responsibility for their own feelings, thoughts, and actions. We were both projecting stuff at one another. The day we started practicing taking responsibility for our individual emotional needs and practicing empathy with one another was the day our marriage started to heal.

What is your core fear?

How do you react when that fear is triggered?

Are you willing to take responsibility for your personal emotional needs and practice empathy with one another?

Chapter 12

REDEMPTION:
HOW WE BROKE GRIDLOCK

Darlena

In the wake of my Divine Love Encounter, I found myself able to approach our marriage from a position of being deeply loved by my Heavenly Father. There could be no doubting it now, after my wild and wonderful ordeal.

> **I must be known in Heaven as one tough nut to crack, because God's done some crazy stuff to chase me down and get my attention.**

Knowing I was loved settled my heart in a secure, unshakable place of resiliency. I might bend, but I won't break as long as I choose to remain in His steadfast love. Establishing this truth is what sustained me when I had to stare-down the rage in my soul without crumbling, take ownership of it, and speak out the shame in confession. It also enabled me to obey God and to do something that was brave and gutsy and trust that I wouldn't be stoned to death when I was done.

That day may have been a public confession in the natural sense, but it shifted something in the unseen realm. It started something rumbling in my life, my marriage, and my home that I would feel the effects of years later. I knew it the moment it happened. When I finished my confession with those last four words, in the spirit, it felt like four individual boulders, falling from my mouth to the ground with a loud, quaking sound as they each hit. Tormenting...Boom! Battle... Boom! With... Boom! Rage... Boom! I sensed that simultaneously taking place in the Courtroom of Heaven was the Great Judge striking His gavel to His bench four times in succession, then proclaiming in a deep resounding voice, "The accused is not guilty!" Bam, just like that, I was liberated from a twenty-year secret that I had relentlessly hid in shame and from the fear of ruining my husband's reputation and my family's lives. Whoa!

The rumble of those boulders falling to the ground created a vibration that traveled all the way to my house and barreled through our front door like the fault line of an earthquake. The rush of liberation swept through our home, redeeming the pain of all the hard years and cleansing the shame of our past. I paid a high price that day for freedom to match the level of torment I had been living in, the misery I'd put my husband through, and the heartache I'd caused my children. The reward, however, was well worth the cost—the payoff was above and beyond what I was expecting in return.

**This time, redemption had now hit our house
and it was glorious watching it work it's magic in our marriage.**

Liberation from shame finally enabled me to end my marriage-long obsession with trying to get Philip to adore me, like my fantasy husband. Wow! Was that ever a relief for both of us. Since the moment I first disappointed him during our first year of marriage, it felt as though I couldn't get him to see me any other way but flawed. No matter what I did to try and please him, or how hard I tried to fit his fantasy, it was never good enough to win his adoration. As long as I perceived that he saw me as flawed, I kept hustling to earn worth and running the treadmill of perfection. For years, it was exhausting trying to get him to see that I was worth loving.

He saw all my defects, all the cracks in my masks, all my posing tactics, all my manipulation and control maneuvers, he knew all my numbing-out habits, he knew all my tricks and all my dysfunctional, insane, undisciplined ways of living. Everything I worked so hard to keep hidden from anybody and everybody outside of our home, he saw no matter how hard I tried to keep it hidden. My pitiful belief was that as long as he saw and knew all my stuff and shame, he would he never love me. The fantasy of perfection drove me to chase after a rabbit that I would never catch, like a greyhound racing dog. It drove me into a raging maniac, until I about lost my mind, then I threw in the towel.

Throwing in the towel was by far the smartest thing I've done. Only then, was Jesus able to rush us with His rescue squads and bring us back to life.

Once I reclaimed my worth, I was able to live inside my marriage and fully participate in it, rather than stand on the outside of it looking in from my hiding place. I kind of liked living inside our marriage. It felt little awkward at first, like when we would intentionally hold hands because it would probably be a good idea or snuggle during a movie because that's what happy couples do. We went away by ourselves in our happy camper for the first time ever, for our anniversary. It felt weird not having the kids with us as a buffer, to be all be all alone for four days, and navigate how to talk without fighting. We weren't fighting, which was amazing, but it's like we didn't know how to be together and be peaceful, like our first year of marriage. Back then, we were ignorant of the dynamics going on, but now we understood. So, we practiced enjoying the peace and being together as best we knew how. I thought at one point, we are alone with no kids, you'd think we'd be having sex like rabbits, but there was hardly any. Something wasn't right.

I ventured, alone, to figure out why things weren't amazing here inside our marriage like I'd hoped, because I didn't want him to know I was disappointed. So, I started picking at Phillip, with judgmental little thoughts like, well if he dressed hotter maybe I would be more attracted to him, or if he practiced a little foreplay sometimes maybe I'd want to initiate sex like he wanted. They were nasty little thoughts that highlighted his faults. I even started noticing things that never bothered me before like his hygiene habits, his eating habits, or his driving habits. What was going on here? Was it because we had been so good at practicing distance and we did for so long, that I didn't notice these things?

Soon, I recognized that I was comparing our marriage to other people's marriage, namely friends. I started comparing Phillip to my friend's husbands. I was convicted of my judgmental thoughts but couldn't stop myself. I also had the grievous realization that I couldn't be happy when something good happened for anyone, not my family or my friends, people that I said I loved, not even Phillip. *Now, there was something way off about that.* It made my toes curl when something good happened to someone that had hurt us in the past or even worse, if I did not think they deserved it. It was like God resigned and someone erroneously made me the Great Judge. I must have wandered over into Wasteland again, unaware. I figured I should find my way home soon, before I started turning green with envy, got stuck in a mire, and totally lost the freedom I'd gained in my life and my marriage.

So, here's how things shook down. About a year after our big rescue, all was well on the home front and I was practicing vulnerability and courage, living seen and known, like Brene' Brown had inspired me to live. Then, I get super hurt by a friend. The unfortunate situation with this friend caused a domino-effect of relational loss, rejection, and disappointment for me. It was one of the hardest things I'd experienced with a friend since in high school. So, I found myself really struggling again, feeling very raw emotionally, fragile, and unsteady—not in a total funk, but accessing the damage and navigating how to move forward.

Phillip had been incredibly sensitive and understanding, plus listened to me talk for hours and hours processing the ordeal, so he was my safe place in the moment. *Now here comes the big **but**.* One Sunday afternoon, he did something that hurt my feelings so bad that I can't even remember what it was. I grabbed my phone and purse and stormed out of the house to take off in the car somewhere until I could calm down.

The thing is, my get-away car is pivotal to my story, so I must pause to paint a mental picture for you. *You're going to love it!* See, the reason we had the vehicle I am about to describe is because our oldest daughter moved away to college, leaving us short one car. To help us solve our dilemma, my sweet momma told us we could have my daddy's old vehicle. So, I flew to Texas to pick up this vehicle and drive it back to Georgia to use until we could afford another car, which I was praying would be real soon. Now mind you, this vehicle used to belong to us when our girls were little, so that should clue you in on how old it is.

When we upsized to the big SUV that hauled our first travel trailer, we passed this vehicle on to my daddy, as he had a strange affection for it. Okay, here's the big reveal. My get-away car in this story is a 2000, hunter green, Toyota Sienna van. It's pretty dinged up, has chipped paint spots all over the front from Texas bugs, and all the door handles are broken except for the passenger side door. That means you have to crawl in and out of the van by hiking over the console, which was a comedy show in itself. My youngest daughter said it looked like a big rolling turd, that's how attractive it was. Needless to say, it was very humbling to drive. Naturally, I always parked very far away from anywhere I drove it. My son asked if I would wait and be late to pick him after school, so everyone would be gone when I came in the van. From our life story thus far, you've probably gathered that we like to give things pet names. We affectionately called this van, the Shame Wagon.

When I climbed in that Shame Wagon that Sunday afternoon, it had been a least a few of years since I'd had an episode of this magnitude, maybe since the trailer park. *Remember the Krispy Kreme and wine meltdown?* So, I guess I was making up for lost time when I drove through Taco Bell and McDonald's and stopped at a remote gas station for a mini pizza, king size Snickers, and large Coke. I pulled into an empty church parking, the tears began to flow, and the food wrappers started coming off. I sat there crying and gorging for at least an hour, hoping to completely numb out before dragging myself back home.

Then, I paused to entertain a thought that high-jacked my pity-party, "What if someone I knew drove up and caught me like this?" I slowly lowered my food and rotated my head all around to see if I was being watched unaware, and answered the question out loud, "I would die of shame." As I heard myself think out loud, I felt that old familiar shame began to pour over me. However, before it engulfed me, I began to pray and repent for my behavior. I begged God to help me understand why I couldn't find contentment and satisfaction in my life with Phillip when we'd worked so hard and come so far. After I'd dried myself up and was bagging up all the empty food containers, I heard these words that I believe were from the Lord.

**"As long as you keep holding up
your fantasy life against your real life,
you will always live in disappointment
and you will never know what it's like to feel REAL."**

I sobered up very quick, threw my trash and leftover junk food away in a dumpster where no one would see me, and wistfully drove home in the Shame Wagon, sunk way down low in the seat. Phillip was watching T.V. when I got home; his numbing out vice. I quietly and shamefully went upstairs to journal and ponder those words. That night I couldn't sleep, so I got up, went into our large bathroom and sat at my cute, seafoam green make-up table, as I typically did when I couldn't sleep.

My mind went back to the scene in the Shame Wagon surrounded by my tears and food wrappers, and those powerful, wise words that came in response to my prayers. I turned on a random worship playlist on my tablet and began to ask God to give me more revelation about my fantasy life and why I couldn't let it go of it. I got my answer, just at the next song was coming on, "Judgment and jealousy hold you captive in your Fantasyland." Of course, I rose up and said, "Well, judgment and jealousy need to go. Lord, deliver me of judgment and Jealousy." With my eyes closed, I prayed and immediately saw an image in my mind of some dark figures that lived inside my chest. In rebuttal of my prayer, I heard them hiss, "We've lived here a long time. If you want us to go, you're going to have to fight!" Before I had time to think, "I have no fight left in me," I notice the lyrics to the worship song playing:

> I hear the whisper underneath your breath
> I hear you whisper, you have nothing left
> I will send out an army to find you
> In the middle of the darkest night
> It's true, I will rescue you
> I will never stop marching to reach you
> In the middle of the hardest fight
> It's true, I will rescue you
> Oh, I will rescue you

It was a Lauren Daigle song I'd never heard until that second. It inspired me to sit up straight and tall and say, "I'm not fighting with you. My Savior has already won the fight. When I'm done praying these prayers I'm about to pray next, you're not going to want to stay!" Out of my mouth came prayers of forgiveness that I'd not been able to pray for the friend that had recently hurt me. Then I began to repent for judging people that I hadn't even realized was judgment. Lastly, I repented for being jealous over good things happening to other people, something else I'd never prayed. While I was praying and my eyes were still closed, I saw an army of angels swoop down from heaven and line up right in front of me. The two dark figures seemed terrified and gripped my insides, as if to hunker down and hang on for dear life. The angels began to tug on the them, but they were hanging onto my heart like two little kids being pried off playground equipment. I wrapped up my repenting by telling Judgment and Jealousy I didn't want them in my life anymore, "Now go, in Jesus' name!" As that command rolled off my tongue, the angels yanked those two gruesome characters out of my chest, flung them over their heads, and they got sucked in a black hole. Wow! That was intense!

Phillip left to fly out of state for a week-long trip before I had a chance to apologize for my behavior or tell him about the bathroom deliverance. I didn't feel any dramatic difference when I woke up in the morning. I just went about my day and sort of forgot about the whole incident. However, as the week progressed, I realized I was seeing and hearing differently than before. I wasn't thinking nasty judgmental thoughts. When I saw certain people that typically triggered me, I didn't feel myself flair up in jealousy. I thought, *wow, this is so cool!* I never even really realized how terrible some of my thoughts and feelings were towards others until they were gone. This was amazing! I thought I'd go to my grave thinking that way, mainly because I thought it was just me, part of my personality. I'm extremely grateful that's no longer the case. The most incredible moment of this breakthrough, however, was when Phillip got home from his trip. When he walked in the door six days later, I saw him so differently, it was shocking. It was like I was seeing him for the first time, like when he walked into Student Services at Regent University and "Love is a Many Splendored Thing" started playing like background music. I don't think my words will do justice to tell you just how he was suddenly transformed through my eyes but is was splendid for sure.

After several minutes of hugging, we went into his office to share my experience with him. Through hot tears, I asked him to forgive me for not seeing him our whole marriage because I looked right passed him when he didn't match my fantasy.

I realized I'd spent our entire marriage standing outside of it looking for something else to bring me contentment and satisfaction, longing for something else to make me happy. I'd spent countless years trying to belong somewhere besides to him and our marriage.

I'd judged him harshly for not treating me like a princess and "adoring" me, like I fantasized, whatever adoring is supposed to look like. I conjured up in my mind what it looked like to be loved, as sick as my family system was, based on my Papaw adoring me and treating my like a Princess and my daddy telling me he loved me and that I was beautiful every day of my life. I combined that with whatever fairy tale made me feel butterflies and whichever love story got me all starry-eyed along with whatever man came packaged like a G.Q. cowboy.

There you have it. That's what Phillip couldn't live up to. I judged him for it, hated him for it, and raged at him for not living up to my fantasy, and most of all for not making me feel loved. I concluded that one of the things that fueled my rage was how I couldn't get him to look and act like my perfect fantasy husband and I was ashamed of our imperfect marriage. Yep, that's an awful lot to put on a person.

Nevertheless, I judged Phillip for not being my fantasy and was jealous of anyone else whose life remotely resembled my fantasy. *No wonder we were miserable for so long.* We judged and punished each other for not living up to the fantasies that were made up in our childhood.

That my friends, was the revelational conversation that turned the tide of our marriage. It was the ultimate rescue mission, straight from heaven, that came in the form of an embarrassingly ugly, little van from Texas, called the Shame Wagon. We gratefully changed its name to the Rescue Wagon and thanked the Lord every time we got in it after that. I've also thanked the Lord for the revelations we've continued to get about our marriage since that day in the office.

Without question, those rescue missions from the Lord are what saved us.

I will spend the rest of my days being eternally grateful to Father God for saving our marriage and I get to spend the rest of my days in REAL love with "my" handsome prince.

I'd like to wrap up this portion of the book with few things I've learned since my breakthrough that have helped me remain grounded inside our marriage and off the treadmill of perfection. The first one came to me while standing in the office talking that day. It was about the Lord saying that if I didn't give up my fantasy, I would never know what it was like to feel **real**. Well, while we were leaning against the bookshelves in Phillip's office, I looked over his shoulder and spotted one of my favorite children's book that I cherish, The Velveteen Rabbit. I recalled the conversation between Rabbit and the Skin Horse in the nursery about being REAL. Here's the excerpt from the book:

"Real isn't how you are made," said the Skin Horse. "It's a thing that happens to you. When a child loves you for a long, long time, not just to play with, but REALLY loves you, then you become Real."

"Does it hurt?" asked the Rabbit.

"Sometimes," said the Skin Horse, for he was always truthful. "When you are Real you don't mind being hurt."

"Does it happen all at once, like being wound up," he asked, "or bit by bit?"

"It doesn't happen all at once," said the Skin Horse. "You become. It takes a long time. That's why it doesn't happen often to people who break easily, or have sharp edges, or who have to be carefully kept. Generally, by the time you are Real, most of your hair has been loved off, and your eyes drop out, and you get loose in the joints, and very shabby. But these things don't matter at all, because once you are Real you can't be ugly, except to people who don't understand." — Margery Williams Bianco, "The Velveteen Rabbit"

I realized, then, what the Lord meant by REAL. He meant that I would never know what it felt like to be REALLY loved. It's only after being loved the you become REAL. People that try to live perfect lives will never know what this feels like, because they're too concerned with looking sharp and kept. After you've been loved for a long time, you begin to look imperfect, but you don't care anymore, because you've become REAL…REALLY LOVED. You won't find love inside a fantasy because nothing about a fantasy is real. When the Lord kept coming after us and coming after us, rescue mission, after rescue mission, we were worn, tired, and a little messy. But we finally looked loved and felt loved and it had made us feel REAL. Imperfect is what living loved looks like, gutsy and gritty, raw and authentic, like it's really been through something. So, perfect love will never be perfect. REAL is the stuff you can hold in your hand right then and there.

Coming to this realization has helped me understand why we both love old things. We love old houses, old furniture, and old cars because they look worn, rubbed, tattered, and distressed. They look like they've really been through something and have a story to tell. Anyone can go out and buy something shiny, new, perfect looking, and almost fake. But it takes time, rubbing, and pressing the wear and tear of the day-in-and-day-out of living in the messy middle that makes you real. That's where the love is.

> **Old represents something that's lasted, has stood the test of time, persevered, and comes out on the other side of the Wasteland. Its roots run deep, and it's not going anywhere. It's the real deal—raw and authentic, never plastic.**

Secondly, I was able to finally see Phillip and our marriage—the man and the marriage that I had long ago laid on the altar of perfection—through the lenses of compassion versus judgment. I finally saw him for who he really was, a man with staying power, who stayed when it would have been easier to leave. That took courage. That's why we even lasted to have that marriage altering office conversation. I see that now and I love him for it. He now looks at me with tenderness rather than fear, which feels indescribable. We now love each other from a deep place, that feels real and lasting, not perfect, sparkly, or pretend.

From this place, we have gathered our hope for the future from the rubble of our past and have set it on our mantle, letting the redemptive power of God continue to lead the way.

I'm not certain, in all honesty, that I REALLY loved Phillip, like the Skin Horse said, until our breakthrough/breakaway from the fantasy of perfection. My focus was on getting him to love me. Just like my epitaph from years ago when I went on to the self-discovery program called Momentus, read, "Here lies Darlena, who spent her life focused on what she could get rather than what she could give." I worked and manipulated that poor man until he was afraid to get near me because I was so desperate to be loved. I went into the marriage with it all backwards. I didn't vow to love him until death do us part but vowed to get him to love me if it killed him. I'd be willing to bet I wasn't the only one with that agenda. It feels like we live in a world starved for love and affection and ravenous to get it any way they can. What a different world it would be, how different our marriages would be, if we looked for people to love instead. It reminds me of a Dean Martin song, which is the inspiration behind this revelation:

"You're nobody 'til somebody loves you, You're nobody
'til somebody cares…Well, you're nobody 'til somebody loves you, So find yourself someone to love."

A third thing I learned that was really hard to accept, yet I knew I
was reading about myself, came when I devoured, *Present Over Perfect*,
by Shauna Niequist. I realized that I was absolutely living for the "Big
Moments"—holiday celebrations, birthday parties, any kind of party
really, even meetings or conferences, anywhere with a crowd, where
I could sparkle and shine, and light up the room, for as long as I had
the energy. If someone wasn't having one, then I would throw it. If
someone had a party that I wasn't invited to, I felt like I might not
ever recover from FOMO.

I loved sending our photo-shop Christmas pictures, because with
a few lights, some smoke and mirrors, I could make our family look
perfectly happy. I fantasized about everything being epic, memorable,
super fun, and exciting with lots of laughter, drama, and action. I
would wrangle and wrestle with my family to get them to cooperate,
get with the program, and make me look good. I needed Phillip to
look and act like we were a happily married couple, at least while there
was company or we were in public, then they could go back to being
their annoyingly imperfect selves.

Although shameful to admit, I also realized I was addicted to
quick charm, mainly because it didn't last long. Like, quick lunch
dates, or working the room at a party. That way I could control the
environment, look my best, and be on my best behavior for just a
short time. I preferred this over the mundane, daily grind of enduring
love that looked like playing with my kids or hanging out with Phillip
in his shed while he worked. Not cool. What I now realize is that I

don't need or want any of that stuff to hang my image on. I actually came to realize that the part of me that raged was raging against all this fake and phony perfect crap. I was screaming to be free of it and just be real, but it was all that I knew and what I fantasized to look like happiness.

Lastly, you have to be willing to go through difficult things, things that don't always feel good or look pretty. You have to be willing to walk through the Wasteland of your soul without quitting on the people you love or giving up in the middle when it gets hard.

**We have to be willing to be
uncomfortable, experience hurt, and endure pain
which is what makes us all inextricably connected
and deeply human.**

It's how we all make it to our Dreamland, by being willing to try and fail or endure suffering without whimping-out, even when marriage isn't fun and games anymore, your spouse doesn't make you feel good or fit your fantasy, and you think you might have made a mistake. It is not for the faint of heart. It requires staying power, like Phillip had. It requires you to be a finisher.

Everyone has a Wasteland we must trudge through to reach a life of destiny in Dreamland. It's the only way out of the perfectionistic world of Fantasy, a path we all must take to find the true meaning and reason for living.

**You can't expect to spend your life in fantasy
and ever know what it feels like to be REAL.**

It's a place without depth or true meaning outside of performance. It's all plastic, smoke and mirrors, and cover-ups to ensure a safe, controlled, and manageable life of certainty. However, the only way Fantasies can become real is on a movie set, where it can be manufactured and fabricated to look perfect. The real love or real life found there is acted out by professional posers and pretenders. It's an unattainable life that will leave you collapsed on the performance treadmill in your own sweat and tears.

Through my journey, I discovered that Dreamland was never about a geographical location, but a place in our souls where life is real, sometimes messy, uncomfortable, and unpredictable. It is so worth the risky trek through your Wasteland to reach. It's where real love and real life are. It's where greathearted people live brave lives without the certainty of happily-ever-after, unlike the princess in the fairy tales. It's a place I was in danger of losing, while I was hustling for Perfect.

Phillip

Our marriage journey has been a wild roller coaster ride. I rode the marriage-cyclone up the tallest peaks and felt the gut-wrenching drop without warning on the other side over and over. It has been a series of twists and turns getting yanked one way and then another. I have felt buzzed with excitement and scary laughter when you know something is about to happen that could be catastrophic. This ride has been anything but smooth and easy. I would have never imagined that it could be so crazy and yet so good. The fantasy doesn't compare to the real experience.

I had no idea that my married life would test me more than living through an emotional warzone as a child. I was blind to how a childhood fantasy influenced my perception of Darlena. She was expected to fulfill something God didn't design her for. The purpose I dreamed up for my wife came from the pain I carried in my childhood. It was her job to erase everything that went wrong in the past. I didn't realize I was expecting her to be an imaginary character in my sad story who was expected to rescue me from tyranny. The pressure I created with my expectations was unfair and burdened her with conditional acceptance.

But Real love set us free. The path to knowing this real love was unplanned. Real love is knowing you're worth the pursuit apart from a performance. The rescuers, as Darlena said it, made a huge difference in my life, too. Wilson's tangible father-love taught me that I was worth rescuing. But the big deliverance for me came when my sin, my judgment of Darlena was revealed. Ironically, I discovered true love in my weakest moment of our marriage. I was determined to fix her anger problem which brought out my controlling nature. The better way to say it was I was trying to fix her anger problem by controlling her with unrealistic expectations. I hated myself for being powerless and weak, but that's when I discovered how real love works. God's love isn't based on us being perfect and deserving His favor. I was requiring Darlena to earn my love. The performance expectations I had for Darlena changed when I discovered that I needed mercy for my struggles. My perception went from expecting her to be perfect to accepting and appreciating her.

I put too much pressure on Darlena to make me feel worthy of my man-card. The day I realized that it wasn't Darlena's job to validate my manhood, I was a freed slave. God was the only one who could supply the foundation for my masculinity. It was as I stared into His face that I found strong love that awakened my courageous, passionate heart. It took me a long time to realize that Darlena was not my main source for security and significance.

My search for worthiness from her
was over the day that I heard God say to me,
"I am your Father and you are My son."

These very simple words provided a foundation for me that gave me something to lean on when our marriage was being tested. I would come back to the Lord and beg Him to change Darlena and He would say, "I am your Father, and you are My son." How did that help? It reminded me that He was watching over me as a good father would his only son. That stabilized me and gave me the feeling that I had what it took to walk through the difficult times with Darlena.

The season I wanted to avoid was the messy-middle, called the wilderness in the Bible. I hated feeling stuck like I was traveling in circles and repeating the same self-defeating patterns. Powerlessness was my core fear. The inability to fix the constant relationship problems haunted me. I thought we would never get out of that desert alive. God made the path, but we had to choose to follow Him. The Lord didn't push us down the road to freedom. I needed courage to fight for a healthy marriage. I wanted to cover up our problems or run from them.

Courage came in the most peculiar ways. I thought when I flexed male authority or pontificated my manly wisdom, that would be enough to get us through the ugly wasteland of emotional pain. Truthfully, most of the time God did something spectacular in or through my wife. Most of our breakthroughs started with her. Her radical encounters with God were a springboard for healing in our marriage. I was surprised by Darlena's tenacity to keep going. I have never met anyone who has worked on themselves more than my wife has. She was a fierce force to be reckoned with, but now her energy isn't used to fight against me but to fight for and with me. The work she did inspired me to be a better man. The way she appropriated grace to her struggles gave me courage to do the same thing.

Darlena

Now to wrap up my final words, I want to leave you with some parting thoughts. Ours was not a riveting hair-raising story of murder, suspense, adultery, lusty secret affairs, or alien abductions, if that sort of thing excites you. We are an average Christian, middle-class, ministry family with normal everyday challenges, which in this day and age makes us boring. We're not sharing our story because we believe we have it all together now, so we can offer the Keys to Marriage Success. We still must work at this thing called marriage ourselves and practice having a sufficient one, knowing that God glories in our weaknesses. Which means we didn't write this book because we have it all together, but because we've gotten up every day for the past twenty-five years and never stopped trying to get make it work. The legacy that we will leave behind for our family and the world is this—WE NEVER GAVE UP. This scripture, which happens to be my favorite scripture, is the inspiration behind our tenacity:

Not that I have already attained, or am already perfected; but I press on, that I may lay hold of that for which

Christ Jesus has also laid hold of me. Brethren, I do not count myself to have apprehended; but one thing I do, forgetting those things which are behind and reaching forward to those things which are ahead, I press toward the goal for the prize of the upward call of God in Christ Jesus. (Philippians 3:12-14 NKJV)

We have discovered one thing that you can hang your hat on, though, it's where real love, true meaning, depth, authentic connection, true belonging and pure joy is found. It's in the ordinary, day-in-and-day-out of life, where it's messy, dusty, quirky, worn, a little flawed, not so cool, and where "everyone" probably won't be. That's where we have found love, connection, and belonging—trudging through the Wasteland of our soul, in the messy middle that lies in between your unreal fantasy and your real dreams—where life can get hard and long and sometimes boring. That's where you become REAL. That's where REAL love is. That's where you'll find what your soul has been yearning for all along. It's in choosing to believe that REAL life is worth the investment to have the deep and lasting, rather than the quick, fake fantasy. Perfect love is there in the midst of your UN-perfect marriage. This quote by Brené Brown sums things up nicely, I think:

"To love someone fiercely, to believe in something with your whole heart, to celebrate a fleeting moment in time, to fully engage in a life that doesn't come with guarantees—these are risks that involve vulnerability and often pain. But I'm learning that recognizing and leaning into

the discomfort of vulnerability teaches us how to live with joy, gratitude, and grace." -Brené Brown

I guess Oral Roberts was right when he pointed at me with his giant finger through the T.V. set, way back when I was a little girl and said something good was going to happen to me. 'Cause it did! I finally found my way to Dreamland and the life I've always wanted… UN-perfect.

Phillip

Wilson Crump spoke these words to me, "I believe in you. You can get up and over fool's hill if you do it God's way."

The principle of grace/favor empowers us to become who we really want to be. We live from God's favor, we don't try to earn it. It's the same in marriage. Live from a connection built upon acceptance. Don't try to force your fantasy upon your spouse. Love them, accept them, cherish them, and you will discover the best treasure in life; knowing love.

Summary

Living and being loved gives you the courage to live seen, known, and unashamed to live un-perfect. One of the revelations that I've had through this entire experience is that so many families live with the same feelings and struggles that we have had. But they live in hiding, in the hope no one will find out. However, they will secretly come to us for help. My encouragement to you is to begin to come out of hiding and confess what's going on inside your homes. Get help. You'll find that you're not alone. That feeling is very empowering, which is one of the main reasons we have written this book; to help inspire you with our stories to have your own breakthroughs while wading through your own Wasteland. So, you can learn to live loved, seen, and known in the middle of your own UN-perfect Marriage, where Dreamland is found. There's a great reward lying on the other side of the risks that will be required to obtain your dreams. Be brave! Become more afraid of never reaching Dreamland than you are of what you will face in the Wasteland.

Are you living with the same feelings and struggles that we have had?

Are you living in hiding, in hopes that no one will find out?

Are you afraid to wade into your Wasteland to find your Dreamland?

What are you afraid of?

Will you come out of hiding and confess what's going on inside your home and get help?

Chapter 13

7 Practices that Healed Our Marriage

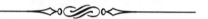

Relationship progress is not line upon line and precept upon precept. Marriage enhancement is not a paint by numbers process. It can be complicated because undesired feelings make our attempts to create connection very challenging. However, we are hard-wired to have love and belonging and we will die trying to find it.

Marriage is messy, ours has been very messy, but we found the deepest love developed in our biggest struggles. Through our discoveries, we grew up and learned practice connection. There are seven practices that healed our marriage.

Number One: *We learned to practice owning our marriage story.* Embracing our reality took a long time because we were controlled by internal mental narratives that said we had to hustle for love. Both of us fantasized about a different married life. We wanted the other person to be more likeable, our circumstances to be easier and more successful, and we wanted out of the story at times. Darlena and I rejected our drama because it reflected our worst selves. The ugly truth was too much for us to accept until we discovered how to apply the real, raw love of Christ.

We couldn't own our story because the fear of not measuring up controlled how we treated one another. Our childhoods taught us how to cover up shame with performances. Darlena desperately tried to please me and I acted like nothing she did was good enough. Acting out "not having what it takes and never good enough" was repeated over and over for most of our marriage.

We didn't know how to break the fear cycle that kept us stuck in this pattern. The light came on for both of us that we were desperately trying to erase our childhood pain by living in a fantasy. The make-believe marriage was two perfect people doing everything right to fulfill one another. I know that sounds absurd, but our efforts to build our relationship were built on illusions that became expectations for one another.

Freedom came when we embraced our reality. Healing started when we recognized that we weren't rock stars or great performers. We had a lot people fooled into believing that we were a power couple with very few flaws, but that wasn't the real truth. The moment both of us courageously accepted the ugliness of our relationship struggles was when we started to heal.

Practice is not a one-time learning experience. Practice is something we try, screw up, and then circle back to clean up, pray about, and try again. For us, acceptance of our mess came as we took off the layers of self-protection and defensiveness that we used to act like we were perfect. The more self-awareness increased the more liberty we gained.

God's grace, His unmerited favor became the catalyst for accepting our story. Christ died the ugliest death known to mankind. His perfect life was given as a payment for our undeserved, ugly, hopeless, imperfect lives. The more we applied His forgiveness to our twenty plus years of failure to do marriage, the more our relationship was healed. We stop hiding our struggles and confessed them out loud to one another, to God, and to others who loved us.

Number Two: *We took full responsibility for our feelings, thoughts, and actions.* We realized that the driving force behind our actions was our personal beliefs. The little narratives that we were listening to inside our heads were causing our unhealthy reactions to one another. Neither of us were literally being controlled by the other person. Nobody was being forced to act up or act out.

Our biggest enemy wasn't the other person, it was fear. Fear was the predator that created disconnection. My fear was not having what it took as a man to lead and her fear was not being loved because she was not good enough. Those fears, once triggered, created a crazy cycle that pushed our buttons to overreact to one another. The fallout was blaming the other person for not measuring up.

Taking responsibility for our feelings and actions started happening when we realized that living controlled by fear was making us powerless. Both of us hated feeling weak and controlled by our emotions. Powerlessness opened the door for us to discover what it meant to be and to act powerful in our marriage. Being powerful meant not blaming the other person for the choices we were making. We accepted full responsibility for the core beliefs that we held to be true.

I believed that I needed to go to the right school, work for the right church, and marry the right girl to find fulfillment in life. That was my fantasy. Darlena believed she needed to be swept off her feet by a prince charming who created the country-club lifestyle for her. These paradigms were causing us to be powerless because we were depending on the other person to make us feel secure and significant.

We took full responsibility for finding security and value in our relationship with Christ. Jesus and Jesus alone could cause us to know abiding security and significance. Marriage was designed to awaken these needs, not be the only source for them.

Number Three: *We learned to practice being vulnerable with one another.* Getting real with one another became a common thing for us. It wasn't about putting one another in place, but more about revealing our deep struggles to each other. We didn't use vulnerability to make the other person feel bad, but it was a tool to invite one another to take a close look at the stuff we were struggling with on the inside.

Vulnerability requires courage. Admitting and confessing your fears, your wants, your hopes, and your flaws is difficult. We started practicing openness fifteen years into our marriage. It was scary to learn about each other at first. I admit that I didn't go first. Darlena led the charge and she was the champion of getting real. I half-heartedly shared stuff to appease her, but when I recognized how free it felt to unload my imperfections, then I became a believer.

We talked about everything including masturbation, sexual dysfunction, spiritual struggles, in-law issues, pain from the past, present fears, ugly moments, kid stuff, and everything in between. The hardest thing for us to be honest about is what we loved about ourselves. It took work to celebrate progress and find acceptance with one another. We learned how to be vulnerable about the things we liked about ourselves and how to celebrate one another's victories.

Number Four: *We learned how to make connection the goal during conflict.* Believe it or not, our fights became our primary source for connection. Both of us came from dysfunctional families that schooled us in how to win fights. Darlena learned how to overpower others with anger. I learned how control others with silence. The weapons of our warfare were used for self-protection not connection.

We didn't realize that if one of us won a fight then the other person lost which meant the relationship was drained.

Other people taught us how to move toward one another during conflict. I was used to running away and Darlena knew how to come at me during a fight. Those tendencies created the opposite of what we longed for. We deeply needed affirmation and validation. Empathy became the tool to save the day. Exercising empathy toward ourselves and our spouse opened the door for connection.

One moment of success set in motion a string of small victories in our communication. One person practicing empathy could deescalate our conflicts into healthy exchanges. Learning to slow down and listen to one another was very helpful. Working on our own self-talk and the narratives that were playing in our heads was huge.

We started to realize that controlling the other person was unnecessary. Our focus became making sure we were making the goal connection during conflict. It would be evident if we were practicing empathy. Eventually, our conflicts turned in to connection because they were learning experiences for both of us.

Number Five: *We learned to practice ministering to our spouse's core needs.* It may seem impossible, but the mouth that hurt you and can be used to heal you. The childhood fantasies that we developed were important markers. The pictures we created in our hearts were held together by words. Those words reflected our deepest desires. Desires are God-given and they reveal our needs. The problem was that we were both expecting our needs to be met in unrealistic ways. I wanted her to be my sexual fantasy and a spiritual mother. She needed me to be a fatherly prince charming. I know, it was sick.

Once we both took away the expectation to have our core needs of security and significance met by the other person, we were empowered to receive from Christ. Those core needs are met in an exchange with the Lord, but our spouse can speak words of affirmation and validation that adds to the work of Christ in our hearts. The words of ministry become like emotional vitamins that bring out our identity. We can't give our spouse an identity, but we can validate it by speaking into their hearts.

We learned to minister to one another during moments of vulnerability. We took turns sharing with one another key edifying words that we felt God had given us to speak to one another. It was transformational for both us. We felt empowered to give encouragement and to receive it.

Number Six: *We learned to forgive ourselves and to forgive one another.* Darlena's struggles were obvious in our early years. She kept apologizing and I kept nodding my head I forgive you. However, I wasn't forgiving her, I was storing up ammunition that I used against her when she lost control of her emotions. Darlena struggled with bitterness because she had an intense hatred for my rejection. The unforgiveness for her was hard to overcome because she felt unloved. Both of us knew the Christian thing to do was to forgive one another, but forgiveness must go deeper than a mental exercise.

Forgiveness should activate an emotional release. It's not working if you don't feel the bad energy of the wound or the offense leaving your soul. We learned that forgiveness was like a surgery on our hearts. We had to dig deep to release the pain or it didn't work. Most of the time, this required prayer and a willingness to allow the Holy Spirit to empower us to let go. We recognized on many occasions that we didn't have the strength to simple say, "I'm sorry or I forgive you," and it was over.

The block to forgiving one another was often an inability to receive forgiveness. Self-hatred was a big part of our childhoods. Self-destruction and self-sabotage were common for us. Believing we deserved to be forgiven and released for our failures was not normal. We had to ask God to help us believe we deserved to be forgiven.

Number Seven: *We learned how to build trust in our marriage.* Trust is like a bathtub full of water. Couples tend to start marriage with lots of trust for one another, a bathtub full of water. We trusted each other very deeply when we started our journey together.

Trust drains out of the marriage because of disappointment and hurt. I'm sure after reading our story you can see that there were plenty of opportunities for us to experience a loss of trust. The bruises we absorbed along the way were intense. Trust was almost completely gone on more than one occasion.

Trust doesn't come back overnight. Our experience was trust returned to our marriage one spoonful at a time. It took intentional effort to restore hope back in our relationship.

The way we restored trust was to believe in redemption. Redemption is the work of Christ perfected for us on the cross. His willingness and faithfulness to continue to forgive us and to restore us provided a way for us to have hope in our marriage.

Summary

Our relationship with Jesus is like a marriage. He is the groom and we are His bride. He is the faithful lover who never gives up on us. We are the imperfect bride that is transformed by His perfect love. He can love us and that gives us an ability to keep learning to love one another.

Rebuilding trust in one another came as we took the risk to fall forward into the loving arms of Christ. He gave us different perceptions of one another's struggles. We stopped seeing the flaws as reasons to divide and started seeing them as opportunities to connect. We stopped using our mouths as weapons to injure and started using them as tools to heal. Before we knew it, our imperfectness that had divided us was now connecting us.

We have done our best to hold nothing back. Our choice to practice vulnerability on this level is not to celebrate our failures. No, we are not proud of how long it took us to mature and heal, but this is how redemption works. Three steps forward and two steps back is progress. I don't think Jesus feared the mess that He knew Darlena and I would make of our marriage. He showed us how to receive His perfect love in our imperfectness. We hope it will inspire you to do the same thing.

CPSIA information can be obtained
at www.ICGtesting.com
Printed in the USA
LVHW010842271219
641829LV00001B/1